ANGELS SPEAK TO ME

ANGELS SPEAK TO ME

A New Age for Mankind

DENNIS WAYNE SCHROLL

InspiringVoices®
A Service of **Guideposts**

Inspiring Voices books may be ordered through booksellers or by contacting:

Inspiring Voices
1663 Liberty Drive
Bloomington, IN 47403
www.inspiringvoices.com
1-(866) 697-5313

Because of the dynamic nature of the Internet, any web addresses or links contained in this book may have changed since publication and may no longer be valid. The views expressed in this work are solely those of the author and do not necessarily reflect the views of the publisher, and the publisher hereby disclaims any responsibility for them.

Any people depicted in stock imagery provided by Thinkstock are models, and such images are being used for illustrative purposes only.

Certain stock imagery © Thinkstock.

ISBN: 978-1-4624-0248-9 (sc)
ISBN: 978-1-4624-0247-2 (e)

Library of Congress Control Number: 2012912380

Printed in the United States of America

Inspiring Voices rev. date: 09/19/2012

TABLE OF CONTENTS

PREFACE

This book provides the background behind my knowledge about God's words of a new age for mankind. A variety of angels, archangels, cherubim, heavenly persons, and God, himself spoke these words to me. Visions that took place over my whole life will explain why and where this age is announced. In summary, this is the new age in which new prophets will bring forward words from God into the world. This is not to replace the old prophecies and Scripture but to fulfill them. For just as the dove brought the leaves of the olive tree back to Noah, so shall the new age bring the Lord back to the world to fulfill his promises. There will be many new miracles as promised by our Lord.

As revealed to me by God over a period of years purposes of these visions are to explain to all how one is saved in Christ, why one must be saved to prevent torment, how it is important to ask God for help in getting to heaven, and how to continue a Christian life with God's support. God has mentioned the temples of the world are lacking and he has provided the reasons for this. He has plans for a new temple for the return of Jesus Christ. God has said, "I will make an altar on earth for justice, truth, and mercy." This has been told to me by an angel and is mentioned in this book. The following chapters are taken from the visions that God did see fit to show me. I do not know why he chose me for these visions, but he refers to me as the "chosen one." I feel this is a huge honor and it is my responsibility to tell others about these wonderful insights into the spiritual world and

God's plans. I know there are many who will desire to know what has been shown and told to me over the years. The angels had told me a number of times to write down what has happened for others benefit. I want to make it clear that there was no special thing I did to receive these visions. I mean, like some sort of mystic session. I only prayed a number of times asking God's forgiveness of my sins and to provide me with a life guided by him. God did mention he said very few have given themselves completely to God as I have. He was glad for this. I made it clear to God and to the world that my faith is strong and it will not be shaken for any reason.

The format of this information is the chronicles of actual events that occurred to me over many years. These following pages are not fiction nor are they stories based on events but these chronicles are detailed accounts of episodes in my life, my visions with angels and what actually happened to me. Chronicling means this is a detailed account of my contacts with angels, heavenly persons and God over my whole life in chronological order for the most part. The angels, heavenly persons and God came to me when I was fully awake and never while in a dream.

Acknowledgement

I wish to thank my mother Mary Ann (Kearns) (Schroll) Kimberling for her hours of effort reading this draft manuscript and making recommendations for changes for clarity and correctness. She proof read two manuscript versions. She is deserving of mention for this very great effort to assist me to make this book as readable and correct as possible. She was the former owner, publisher and editor for many years of a weekly newspaper in Jamesport, Missouri called the "Tri-County Weekly." My sister Rebecca (Kimberling) Lang of Paola, Kansas also contributed time to proof reading the draft manuscript and I also wish to thank her.

INTRODUCTION

Preamble

Originally this narrative was written January 2012, but it has been revised many times as the book was edited. The notes with the many details of my many visits and visions by angels have been written throughout my life.

When I was a child, I had numerous dreams of designing a rocket that could take people to the stars. The mysteries of the universe would be revealed a bit at a time. To begin my dreams I had a small refractor telescope. I often looked at the planets, moons, stars, and galaxies and I dreamed of what it would be like to visit them and discover their mysteries.

As I grew up, I earned Bachelors and Masters Aerospace Engineering degrees from several universities. I was offered a job which I accepted. I worked for the United States Air Force for 40 years at Wright-Patterson Air Force Base, Ohio. This education and job, however, did not completely satisfy my dreams.

In 1973 just three years after the United States Air Force hired me; I began to have answers to my hopes and dreams from the creator of all the universe through visions with many of God's angels. God must have understood my strong desire to know the answers to these secrets as God did send to me many visions. These visions took the form of many different angels and heavenly persons. They visited me numerous times and told me wondrous things that were beyond all my imagining and dreams. A number of times the angels lifted my spirit body from my physical body to take me to heaven, hell and places within the universe. I was also shown future and past events in vivid detail. I prayed to God to reveal to me some of the mysteries of the universe. He answered my prayers but he also showed me many other revelations that I did not ask about. I offered my service to my Lord, and he answered me by giving me one of the greatest tasks one could imagine. I was chosen to bring to the world the details about the future age of mankind and to provide details about the preparations for the return of Jesus Christ. At the time, it was not clear to me why God was providing me all this information. Still, years later it is still not clear to me why he did this. I mean, why he chose me.

Since I am now older and wiser, I have come to realize that God has been giving me messages that were for all the people of the world. He wants other persons in the world to realize the situation the world is now facing. This includes why we should believe in God and why some people should change their ways to show favor in God's eyes. God wants all peoples of the world to be saved from Satan and the damnation of hell. I have therefore committed myself to putting all my notes and poems into a book and to share these messages with all who wish to know about my experiences. I have provided as much detail as humanly possible so that all would experience the full extent of what I saw and heard. I took great pains to provide accurate experiences even to the point of praying to God on some points which I was not completely certain about. God answered my prayers that are for his good works which are included in this book.

The Gift of Vision of the Angels and Heavenly Persons

First and foremost, I ask for God's forgiveness in the delay of getting his messages to the public. My health problems certainly had a lot to do about why it has taken so long. These messages or visions came to me most often between the spring of 1973 and summer of 1986. I was officially *"saved" i*n the spring of 1973. This is when the majority of visions that were mind-bendingly spectacular, came from God and his angels. I was baptized when I was only a baby, but in my mind I chose God in the spring of 1973. I have seen angels since I was a child. I have continued to see angels up until my step-father's funeral in 1997. I have not seen an angel since that time.

The angels have visited me numerous times. The angels and other spiritual characters usually speak to me. This book will give others a chance to know what the angels and spiritual persons have done and what they said to me. I have investigated and learned that it is rare when angels visit a person and that person actually sees them in detail. It is especially rare if the angels speak to a person. I have chosen to share this gift of visions so that all who want can see and hear what I saw and heard. I have been sickly since childhood, nearly dying a number of times. The angels have always saved me from death. That is why I feel a special connection with God and his angels.

You may be thinking -- *Who is he to think he can speak for God? He has not even got a ministerial degree. Is he just making all this up?* Well, believe me; I have also questioned these visions as to whether they are real or just made up in my mind. God had already been one step ahead of me about this. He gave me visions of future events and places not seen by men that later happened and became known. As the angels showed me future events, these events came to pass exactly as they had shown me. Each time I came to believe more and more this all was very real. The angels had asked me to write down these visions and make them available to all other persons of this world. God and his angels' messages are for everyone and not just me. That is why I perceive that God has taken great pains to ensure I believe in these visions and words. The following terms that heavenly persons had for me are given throughout this book and are given in the order in which the angels and heavenly persons used them: the *"chosen one,"* the *"first prophet"* of a new age, the *"messenger"* who was prophesized several thousand years ago in the Bible, and a *"soldier in the Temple of God."*

My wish is that all who read and believe what I've told will gain more faith in God and have eternal life after death. I'm a scientist first and foremost, I thought about the facts of what I had seen and heard. I tried very hard to write them down as accurately as possible. I think this is a very huge responsibility, so it should be as correct as I can make it.

Some may wonder how I could remember so much detail especially in some cases many years after the vision. It is not as difficult as you might think to remember these visions and words. Because this came from God and his angels, it seemed to be branded into my mind and unforgettable. Also, when I think about these events and details when I'm writing them down, it is as if the angels show the event again but in my mind. I can see God wants all this to be written down as accurately as possible. That is important to me also, because I believe many people will study these words to the finest detail so they can be sure they understand the complete meaning of what God and his angels were telling me. The most important things in my mind are that God is teaching me first and secondly he is also giving me wisdom beyond that of the Bible and other ancient writings. I see this as God's words for more recent values he wants us to consider in our lives, all under God's wisdom. In other words, I believe God wishes to update information like that in the Bible or supplement it for the modern world. Information in the biblical times is important and should still be followed, but new words from God, which are more recent, reveal that he is still with us and is watching the world.

The New Age of Mankind

God is revealing his plans for the future of mankind and what angers him or pleases him. As I once stood face-to-face with our Lord, I have an up to date impression about him. I also believe that I have more information about God's appearance and personality than many past prophets have seen or have revealed. I have seen that he is a never ending compassionate person and he overflows with never-ending love. Hate does not ever come from our Lord. Even when prophets say that

God is angry, his anger is guarded for the compassion and care of his people. His angels glow with the light of love and compassion always. They also teach us to be better persons under God's laws and wisdom. I have known the most gentle compassion and forgiveness from our Lord. It is unlike anything from another person. I think people should keep this in mind when interpreting the many words about our Lord.

In conclusion, I have put off too long releasing this information. In addition to my health problems I also feared persecution. Would people say that I am a false prophet? I know false prophets are mentioned in early *Scriptures*, but they always seek to lead people away from God and Jesus. I seek to lead people to discover God and Jesus and the Holy Spirit. I pray to God and Jesus that they forgive me for my fears of retribution. I have since learned that when one walks the path of a true Christian, one must always deal with persecution from men and women when their minds are not open to God's Holy Spirit. There is also the persecution and tricks that Satan and his demonic angels generate. May our Lord give me the wisdom to tell you all this information as honestly and accurately as humanly possible without any evil influence.

I also wish to explain that in all cases these visions occurred when I was fully awake and some visions occurred when I had just awakened. Angels have even put their hands on me to force me to kneel or to prevent my being harmed. I have attempted to include the visions in chronological order. Some of the visions concerning the Temple of God occurred at a later date but I placed them in the early date sections because they are the prelude to the chapters detailing God's new Temple. God explains why present day temples are not adequate anymore for his purposes and why a new temple is necessary. Additionally, some poems may not be in order because they seemed more appropriate in the sections I placed them. I felt the poems were directly from the angels, because when I write poems at other times it is difficult and cumbersome to do. When I wrote these poems, they came to the pen and paper in a matter of a few days very soon after the visions. It was if the angels were singing these poems to me.

Chapter One

Background on Seeing into the Spiritual World

This was originally written January 20, 2012 but the draft was revised a number of times to improve it. Ever since I was a young boy, I have been able to see into the spiritual world. I freely told this to my family and friends. I thought it was something very interesting to talk about. I cannot possibly recount all the times I've seen spirits or "ghosts," as many call them. I have been seeing spirits many times. Sometimes, the seeing or vision would be a haze with a voice and with an emotional impact given to me. Other times, I would see actual people who were the spirits. I knew they were spirits because I could see right through them. At times, the seeing would be so strong that the ghosts would be almost real looking and solid. Strangely enough, I do not ever recall seeing a ghost in the homes where my immediate family lived. When I was married my wife and I had lived in three homes in the Dayton area. We always took great pains to ensure there were no evil spirits living in the homes we chose. If there were spirits in a home that I lived in I would not have any peace. Usually I could immediately tell if the house was haunted or had spirits living there.

The Haunted House

Once when I was about 12 or 13 years old I was staying at my grandmother's house in Jamesport, Missouri. The house has since been demolished years ago in 1970 and replaced by a smaller home. The brick house was a large 2 story brick home. It was not brick veneer, but brick that was 4 courses thick.

Author's note: Reference Jamesport Tri-County Weekly newspaper, dated Thursday, January 29, 1970. This was one of the oldest houses in Jamesport being built in the 1870s. The house was built by Isaiah H. Jones and Amelia C. Jenkins who were married July 27, 1869 in Jamesport. The Daviess county history says that Mr. Jones was one of the town's prominent men and was on the board of trustees of the corporation of the City of Jamesport which was incorporated August 6, 1872. He was very successful with his Great Western Flouring Mill. This prominent and wealthy Jones family resided in this brick house. They were the parents of two children, Adria A. and William Isadore. When their daughter was in her teens, she died in one of the upstairs bedrooms and for many years, the bedroom was left untouched and a stranger was never allowed to enter the bedroom in which she died. Thus began the story of the haunted house. Following this time the Jones' were grieved very much and the house was closed in with a high fence and heavy wooden doors were on the east and south which many say were never opened during the time the Jones remained there following their daughter's death.

I and my brother, Terry, slept in the spare bedroom on the second level to the right as one faces the front door of the home. I was awakened in the middle of the early morning hours hearing crying and sobbing noises. I thought it was my brother so I was concerned for him. I grabbed his shoulder only to find out he was sleeping and I had awakened him. I could still hear the crying and sobbing of a young child. It continued for a few minutes so I got out of bed to go tell my uncle who slept in the back of the house in his bedroom. After I got him out of bed he came to the room with me, but by that time the crying and sobbing had ended. Well, I just went back to bed and fell asleep with no further noises.

In the morning I came downstairs to breakfast and I remember that grandma had made bacon, eggs and toast. I could smell this on my way down the stairs that were in the center of the house. After I sat down and began to get my breakfast, grandma spoke to me, "I hear from my son that you heard crying and sobbing in that room last night." I replied, "Yes, it was a bit spooky when I discovered it was coming from the room and not my brother." Grandma said, "I've heard the story that two young children were in that room many years ago and they were very ill. The story is that one died in that room from an illness." She said, "I think it was in the 1890's." I stated, "Wow that is some story isn't it." She said, "A few others have heard the crying and sobbing also. My sons don't want to sleep in that room for that reason." I replied, "But you put me in there." She said, "We hoped you would be alright. I'm sorry." I replied, "Well, at times I wish I could not hear and see ghosts. It scares me at times!" I found out later that this was the same room that Adria A. Jones died.

Another Haunted Farm House

As a high school student, I often took jobs on surrounding farms for some spending money. Once I was offered a job to help my friend who had a farm about 15 miles south of Jamesport. We had gathered up his father's hay with his Ford tractor. He pulled the flat bed wagon with hay along side this abandoned house on his father's property to unload. I jumped down and walked into the house because we had to pick up the bales of hay by their twine and carry them into the rooms of the house. My friend threw the bales down off the wagon and I would pick them up by the twine with both hands. I carried them into the house and stacked them into the bedrooms on the far part of the house. When we finished filling these rooms, it was time to fill up the living room nearby the wagon. We had been walking through this room. I took back several bales and began to stack them against the far wall in that living room. I had set down several bales on the floor. But, when I took back the next bale of hay and began to sit it down, I saw a misty area that resembled a small cloud about 2 to 3 feet above the floor. Immediately, I saw into the middle of this mist a very angry face that stared at me. It was a horrifying face that looked at me like it wanted to kill me. I saw the eyes, nose and mouth as this moved quickly towards me. I did not have time to move aside so it went right through my chest. As this happened I heard a piercing scream that made my bones shake all over. After the spirit passed through me it was as if it drained all the energy from me. This made me feel weak and ill. I had to sit down outside. I knew I could not go back into that room again.

My friend finished the job of stacking the bales in that room without further incident. As we headed back to the hay field, he told me a story about the people who used to live in that home back in the early part of the twentieth century. It was about a man who terrorized his wife and one day he killed her on the couch with a large kitchen knife. He put her body behind the couch. He then committed suicide on that couch. The location of the murder and suicide was at the same place where I saw the angry spirit. My friend told me that for years no one would live in that house until the owner of the property finally sold it to a family who were unaware of this story. The family heard all sorts of screams and objects moved about. After only a short time they moved out of the house before this drove them mad. Since that time, no one would live in that house. My friend said I must have seen the ghost of that man as he was quite mad. This is another example where I had a vision of a ghost. This time I was attacked by the ghost. This became a more serious affair for me to consider. I begin to worry more about these spirits I saw.

Evil Spirits Haunt Me in Dayton, Ohio

When I moved to Dayton, Ohio in June 1970 for my new job with the United States Air Force, I looked forward to starting a new life. My life was interesting and without incident in the first two apartments in which I lived so I was happy again. Maybe I would even get married soon. My thoughts were that I now have time to look for a woman whom to date. Things changed dramatically when I moved into my third apartment in Huber Heights, Ohio. Evil ghosts and spirits began to trouble me and they made my health worse on each passing day. It was odd that these rooms would be haunted by evil spirits since these apartments were relatively new. I began to get ill and feel very terrible once again as I had when I was a child. I finally realized that if I could not rid myself of these evil spirits they might make me extremely ill or even cause my death. I needed a way out of this problem.

I purchased a number of books and began to read about my situation. Being a Christian, I read the Bible as well. I thought there might be some useful advice in these books if I just looked earnestly and long enough. Finally, a remarkable stroke of genius hit me regarding an idea I got from the Bible. I could rid myself of these terrible spirits if I asked the angels and God to take them away from me. After all, the Catholic Priests have been taking evil spirits from people for years. It is recorded in the New Testament that Jesus took evil spirits from people. I prayed often and asked God to rid me of evil spirits and give me back my health. After several months of asking, God answered my prayers. These visions of evil spirits disappeared. However, they were replaced by visions of angels. I even had an extensive vision with many events when my spirit body was lifted to heaven. This I recalled in detailed chronological format in the following chapters. Most of these visions occurred before I met my wife and I was married in November, 1973.

Angels Visit Me But Evil Spirits Still Haunt Me.

There were episodes of seeing ghosts even after my marriage. I would see angels up to that time but other ghosts and evil spirits as well. In the late 1980's, my wife and I moved into a new house south of Tipp City in Deer Cliff Run. The home was built to our specifications. Our marriage became more troubled while we lived in that house.

My wife got a legal separation. At that house some evil spirits had attached themselves to me and they tormented me quite often. They caused my health to degrade again. This was a new home with no history of ghosts or so I thought. I especially had two houses built to ensure there would be no spirits to torment me. In this house these evil spirits tried to terrorize me until I could stand it no longer. Years later, after I had asked God for help to rid me of evil spirits I began to have new problems with them again. Often, I saw a demon that was black all over with small horns and red eyes that glowed. It would often look into my windows to frighten me. I was "*saved*" back in the spring of 1973, but it seemed to me that my faith was faltering so the evil spirits were coming back.

In addition to the evil spirits, the angels were also constantly visiting me with advice. They were insistent that I write down these heavenly visions and the spoken counsel of these heavenly angels and persons. The angels also told me to write down more about the visions that happened years ago in 1973. They said they would help me to remember. This I did and, after some time writing down these visions, my health and state of mind began to improve. I have included the words about these visions in the following chapters. I wrote down the dates of the visions and the writing of these visions separately to make more sense about the order of revelations given to me since there are many different incidents of visions. All of this led me to attend church again and the angels came to me and said they are pleased.

Haunted House in Dayton, Ohio with a Family of Ghosts

Not all the ghosts I saw were terrible spirits. After I and my wife got back together we moved into our third home in 1986 in the Dayton View Triangle, Dayton, Ohio. This was an older home and we both spent many hours renovating it. Here we visited with many new neighborhood friends. My wife did a lot of volunteer work for Dayton and so we got to visit a lot of her friends as well. Once we went to some friends' home in University Row which is another nearby Dayton neighborhood. As we sat in their living room and chatted, I could after twenty minutes see several ghosts walking about their home on the first level. They were dressed like a family in the 1890s. The wife kept walking into the kitchen and then the hallway by the living room where we were sitting. Soon a young boy and girl came down the stairs and the mother and father came to the living room next to the front entry door to see them off to some other place, maybe to school I am thinking. I told my friends about this and they were elated to have ghosts in their home. It appeared these were friendly ghosts of persons who had not moved on to heaven or hell. I did not hear these spirits say anything.

I hope this information will help others with no faith or weak faith in God to find a renewed faith. Heaven, God, spirits of heaven and angels are all very real to me. A person needs to realize that these worlds exist together. That is, the earthly world and the spiritual world exist side by side. We cannot live in the earthly world without paying our respect and reverence to the heavenly spiritual world as well. The price that we will pay upon death is just too great. I mean the everlasting loss of our soul to damnation and hell. So I pay my respects to the reader of this book by thinking of your welfare. It is my desire that you ensure your lifestyle and frame of mind about God be positive and that you be saved in Jesus Christ our Lord. Please remember to pray to God and those in heaven with a proper respect. I ask that you pray to God to be saved so you too may live eternally in heaven. I have learned that with great faith in God and his angels you can have wonderful happiness here in this world as well.

CHAPTER TWO

VISIONS REMEMBERED WHEN
I WAS A CHILD

September, 1956 (Note that the date of the vision will be included under the chapter title in the remainder of this book.)

I wrote about this vision on March 4, 1986. The first vision I recall having with angels occurred in 1956 when I was in the fifth grade or 10 years old. It was in the early fall before the tree leaves turned to colors. I went to class at the grade school in Lock Springs, Missouri at the beginning of the school. Before this I attended a one room school house named Clear Creek School that was located in the woods. This was within walking distance from our farm home. Neither of these schools is in use today. My fifth grade teacher was punctual and sharp on discipline. Up to this time I had turned in my school home work papers to my teachers with the name Dennis W. Kimberling, the surname of my new step-father. I was young and did not really even think about what my last name was supposed to be. I only knew my new step-father's last name was Kimberling. Well, the fifth grade teacher protested to the whole class that my name was really Dennis W. Schroll. She embarrassed me greatly in front of the whole class and so I felt badly. I had this feeling that I was abandoned by everyone, school and family.

My father, Wayne Max Schroll died in a plane crash of a PT-29 Navy training plane near Hutchinson, Kansas when I was but 2 years and 10 months old. He had just gotten his pilot's license. After he died, my mother Mary Ann remarried another man, Lewis Edward Kimberling. Because this teacher had embarrassed me in this way, I felt that I was not part of our new family. This greatly distressed me for several weeks. I became depressed and I began to take long walks alone into the fields and woods near our farm house. The farm was located about 5 miles south of Jamesport, Missouri.

One day I walked about one half mile south of our farm house to a grassy meadow with large trees on slopes that overlooked a small creek. This was on our neighbor's property, but it was my favorite place. I had a thinking spot that was under this one very large tree where two years earlier I had spotted a herd of 10 to 15 deer running away. This spot was also along the path that I walked in the past to the one room country school house. The tree and meadow was a very familiar and a comfortable location for me to visit and think.

Feeling abandoned and despondent I sat down under that tree. The air smelled sweet and full of flowers. The birds sang many tunes that were like music to my ears. Here I prayed to God that he bring back my father Wayne Max Schroll. I needed to talk to him about my problems at school. At this young age I did not understand that this was not possible. To my astonishment an angel of the Lord with the look of concern in his face appeared in front of me saying, "Why do you weep, little one. Our Lord Jesus knows your father and has kept him for you. Your father does love you greatly, but he is not of this world anymore. He will help us to look after you." In my heart I was happy to hear these words, but I shouted to the angel, "You can never take the hurt away!"

The angel looked greatly distressed and began to put his hands together as in prayer. He was in a robe of white that glowed greatly as it must have had a light within. He raised his hands to heaven and reached upward. Before, his wings were folded back behind him and only visible above his shoulders and to his sides. I gasped as I saw his wings spread outward and then upward as he moved upward as to fly. The wings extended at least six feet to each of his sides. He ascended upward out of sight toward the sky above in a large beam of white light.

I was looking upward at this marvelous sight, when to my surprise I was aware that I was not alone. I saw two more different angels on each side of me. One of them reached a hand to me and with a most sincere expression said, "We love you very much." I said to them, "What does love mean? I know the pain and the hurt of being unloved." Then each one of them put a hand on my shoulders and I could feel a warm glow within me. Peace and contentment were within me then. My cares seemed to melt away. There was no more pain and sorrow at that time. They took their hands from me and the feeling left me, but not entirely. To this day, which is about 55 years later, I feel the presence of that Spirit within me and it always feels most comforting.

The two angels said, "We will instruct you for our Lord's namesake for he has felt your sorrow and pain and loves you very much. Your prayers will not be left unanswered." These angels had white robes that glowed like there was a light within them. They had wings that reached above their heads which were of golden yellow and their wings folded back behind them visible only at the sides. They began to sing praises in most heavenly voices. Originally the songs were beautiful but unrecognizable to me as they were in a language unknown to me. They sang one final song to me that I understood.

> "How can the Lord come into your heart?
> When you are near him you are a part
> Our Lord does love you very much
> For you he died and gave very much

God, our trumpets sing praise to thee
We always want to with you be
And Lord why cannot this boy see?
That you will love and protect him through all eternity

Praise our Most High God Almighty
He is Lord in the heavens and Most High ... Amen ... Amen"

My comment then was, "Well, I believe in God but why would he be so interested in me?" The angels both shouted, "Hallelujah! Hallelujah! Hal...le...lu...jah.......(Hal-lay-lou-yah)!" They said, "It is only enough that you believe." As I sat by that tree with an angel on each side of me, they took turns saying the following:

1. "Blessed is he who is sorry and seeks forgiveness for his sins, for he is forgiven by our Lord Jesus.
2. Blessed is he who is soft spoken and patient for he is a gem in God's eye and a pleasure to keep company with.
3. Blessed is he who loves all women and takes care of them, for their burden in life is greater to carry than a man's. God will find a special place for those who care for women as they would properly care for themselves.
4. Blessed is he who loves all the children of earth and protects them from evil for they do not know the evils of the world and they are instinctively good and honest to all.
5. Blessed is he who follows our Lord Jesus and keeps him in his mind as a shining example to live his life by, for God will save him from his sins and he will live in heaven through all eternity.
6. Blessed is he who is good and compassionate to all others, friend and enemy, for his reward will be the similar favorable treatment to him by our Lord multiplied by ten.
7. Blessed is he who walks with love, loving God greatly, loving others and loving thy own self, for he will be rewarded with much praise by our Lord and his angels.

8. Blessed is the heart that always seeks to give rather than take, for he will be rewarded many times over for all that is given.
9. Blessed are the peacemakers and abstainers of the crime of war and violence for they will be exalted as most holy persons.
10. Blessed are the hard workers and diligent honest working persons for they will be honored.
11. Blessed is he that gives justice and does not cheat or lie for they will be judged likewise by our Lord with honest justice.
12. Blessed is he who would do unto others with kindness as he would have them do unto himself for our Lord will remember their kindness."

The angels again spoke, "These are the great examples to live by and the promise of blessings from our Lord when you follow these words. Do not worry if you stray along the road in life because our Lord will be with you and he will send angels to look after your well being."

The angels then put their hands together as in prayer and raised their hands and arms heavenward. A brilliant silver glowing light shone down on all of us. A host of heavenly voices from a choir sang out. I was blinded but caught a glimpse of them as they ascended upward to the sky. They turned their heads to me and said, "Remember what we say and that God loves you." I went home with a new resolve to meet life head on and be blessed by God. I was blinded for the rest of the afternoon until evening when I could see again. In the following days, it seemed that everyone looked at me differently after this. It was as if I had something within me that attracted them and they wondered what it was. After this I firmly believed in God and his angels. I felt my faith was strong and nothing would ever take it away from me.

I never told anyone about this incident until much later in my life. In fact, my memory of this incident was very vague in 1986 when I wrote these words. The words and images came back to me as I wrote them down. This startled me that I could recall so much because before this it was not so vivid to me. My only thought was that the Holy Spirit must want me to record this for others. Anyway now it is completed.

In Jesus Christ I pray as I commit this event and words spoken to the written word to be true and honestly given. Amen.

CHAPTER THREE

AN EARLY VISION AS A CHILD

June, 1958

I wrote about his vision on March 15, 1986. When I was eleven years old and in the fifth grade at a small country school in northwest Missouri, I lived with my parents, brothers and sisters on an 80 acre farm. My favorite pastime was to take hikes into the wooded area about one-quarter mile south of the house and adjoining barn. The wooded area went back some distance. It was laced with creeks and hills. Many of these creeks were small streams and had embankments overlooking the twists and turns. I could easily cross the creeks in the daytime while walking back into the woods. There were many places in the creek beds that were full of rocks. My passing across these creeks was easily accomplished by walking on the rocks in these streams.

One time my brothers and I decided that we were old enough to go camping and stay overnight. We packed food and cooking pans and dishes into old army packs. We headed out into the woods one summer afternoon. These packs were olive green being World War II Army surplus packs. We couldn't afford a tent so we made a lean-to from tree branches and hoped the leaves would shed any rain. Actually, we felt quite confident that we were explorers having made this lean-to ourselves. The lean-to was very nice to sit back into after a meal cooked over a campfire of wood. We could relax in the shade for awhile. Later as evening approached, we made our beds from old army blankets we also brought with us and we retired for the evening. These olive green woolen blankets were World War II Army surplus as well. It was nice to lay back, talk and look at the evening stars.

As the evening wore on, the increased darkness revealed that clouds were moving into the sky. It was soon apparent that some type of storm was moving in as we could hear thunder and see lightning in the distance. The lightning flashes were frequent. The storm was eerie and interesting to watch as the frequent lightning moved towards us. We did not have concern for our situation at that time. As the storm got closer, a strong wind began to blow and this tore down part of the lean-to we were trying to sleep under. We soon realized our danger and in the darkness of the evening we made haste to collect our goods and we threw them into our packs. Just at that moment as we were ready to leave, it began to rain in torrents. We were all in a panic because we were kids. We began to run through the woods towards the house. This was about one fourth mile through the woods and one fourth mile through a pasture. Since I was the oldest and strongest, my brothers ran behind me as I ran head long into the darkness through the brush and between the trees. The silhouettes of the trees were visible on each lightning flash. The bushes were not so easy to make out so I got tangled in some of the bushes.

Suddenly, I felt a solid hand on my chest stopping me almost immediately. It was as if invisible hands were laid on my shoulders and chest from the front so that I could not move forward any more. I looked downward at some light which at first had the appearance of a very large candle. Then the rain slowed down to a sprinkle. After my eyes focused, I saw a person with wings wearing a robe. The person was lit from within like a glow candle. My brothers stopped behind me and they wanted to know what was wrong. I looked downward again and I was startled to see that the lighted person was really an angel with its wings stretched upward very much. I heard a deep voice proclaim, "Thou guardian shall watch thee and protect thee from harm." When I looked downward more it was amazing to see during a lightning flash a fifteen foot drop off into a pool of water and rocks in the creek. When the next lightning flash illuminated the entire area, words could not express my shock. I was seeing a near disaster I had just been saved from. I told my brothers and then exclaimed, "Wow, we almost fell into the creek bed!" On the sand and gravel bar across the water the angel still was there. He looked at me with much care and compassion or so it appeared to me. He was in a light blue gown and had wings that arched outward from his shoulders and reached upward to about seven feet above the top of his head. He said to me, "Yea are my children. I love you very dearly." The angel stood there in all its magnificence through several lightning flashes. I looked in awe at the silver and gold glow all about the angel. He was tall with very large wings. I would guess he was at least 7 feet tall to the top of his golden hair. His hair was braided upward and it flowed downward about his shoulders. Then I noticed the angel had a golden vest open to the light blue gown in many places. His feet were adorned with golden slippers. When another lightning flash came the angel was gone.

This all was very shocking to me but seeing the angel calmed me down a lot so that I no longer feared the storm. I and my brothers walked around to a crossing in the creek and we managed to make our way to the pasture by carefully walking only when we could see. We then ran through the open pasture up to our barn lot. As we entered the barn lot, it began to pour rain again very hard. After we reached the barn and shelter from the rain we rested in the milking room until the rain slowed down. I and my brothers went to the house, pulled off our wet clothes and we went to bed. I do remember looking into my pack and seeing a lot of broken eggs. What a mess! That angel certainly saved me and my brothers from harm and possibly even saved our lives.

Several weeks later my brother Terry was raccoon hunting with a friend. They were near his friend's farm on the other side of Lock Springs, Missouri and were running down a raccoon with their coon dogs when a strange thing happened to them. They said it was as if they ran into an invisible wall. They looked down to see a 60 foot cliff drop away. The angel saved their lives that night also. They did not mention to me whether they saw an angel. Maybe they did and did not want to mention it for fear they would not be believed. The Lord again sent an angel saving my brother!

**My guardian angel's appearance as he stood
in a creek bottom on a gravel bar**

CHAPTER FOUR

I AM SAVED! VISION OF THE ARCHANGEL GABRIEL AND OTHER HEAVENLY HOSTS

March, 1973

I wrote a complete narrative of this vision years later on March 28, 1986 from many loose notes that were recorded soon after the vision in March, 1973. My first vision of the Archangel Gabriel and visions of heavenly hosts was written in May 1973. As I pieced together the chronology of the vision God opened up my mind and I recalled more of this fantastic vision. That enabled me to fill in the gaps missing from the loose notes.

When I was a child I was fortunate that our family lived on a small farm with nature just out the back door. I was very happy at that farm. I liked the animals and trees and the other things in our environment. When I reached high school I was growing so fast that I felt much pressure from the increasing responsibilities given to me. I rebelled some about this and so I think I lost my way. I felt chained to so many responsibilities that I did not desire. When I graduated from high school, this afforded me the opportunity to get away from any school and my family for awhile. I moved to El Mirage, Arizona which is near Phoenix, Arizona. I stayed there with my grandmother Leona

Kearns and two of her sons Walter and Bob. I had two uncles who were nearly my age and we did many interesting things together. When the summer days of my visit were finished, I decided to stay in this area longer as I liked Phoenix and the southwest very much. My uncles said I must get a job if I was to stay with them any longer. My uncle Bob found me a job in Scottsdale, Arizona and I worked there a few months. Then I found another job at the same newspaper where my uncles Walter and Bob worked when I quit this first job. I quit because I was the only one there and I believed the man who ran the shop was always away drinking liquor. I worked in Glendale, Arizona for about nine months with my uncles and this provided me with happiness until I was let go.

After this I drove back to Jamesport, Missouri to be with my family. I decided it was time to go to college and get better work. I also again had the desire to learn. I went to Central Missouri State College, Warrensburg, Missouri for two years where I really enjoyed science, physics and mathematics. I decided this college did not afford me the opportunities I desired so I transferred to the University of Missouri at Rolla, Missouri. There I studied physics and mechanical engineering and I finally settled on aerospace engineering. I put three years of hard work to graduate on the honor roll. I desired a job in propulsion research and so I took the job offer given to me by the interviewing representative from the United States Air Force, Wright-Patterson Air Force Base, Ohio. I became unhappy again when I was placed at a job involving crew systems which was not my desired area of science to work. I finally settled down with this work after a few years and I tried to do my best.

In my personal life I made friends and dated a few women. I decided that I needed to know more about people and society. I studied philosophy and religion for about two and one-half years on my own by reading. I put much study and thought into religion. I decided that faith in God was important for ultimate happiness. I believed deep down in my heart in God but I was unhappy for some reason. I could not seem to have a happy life. I was frustrated about this and I desired to know the answer. What did Jesus and Moses know that I didn't, that would allow personal happiness. One evening in March of 1973 I was thinking about the answer to this concern. I reached deep into my soul to know God. I wanted to know him and be accepted by him and other people. I prayed so much and I believed strongly in God but I had much to learn about life and happiness. I had been praying to God the answers to some of my questions for several months. Finally, after I had not received any kind of answer, I prayed that I would agree to place my life and my soul in God's hands. That is, if he would show me the way. I asked with deep conviction for his assistance to find my way.

At that time, my life changed forever. Heaven opened up to me.

And an angel descended from heaven
On a starry rainbow of love
And with our Lord were seven
Who had come to me from above

I was engulfed with understanding
And the desire to know was answered
God revealed what he was planning
And the universe was revealed to me

The Archangel Gabriel glowed with open arms
And declared with love "You are saved!
Understanding you will have of the Bible
Your enemies will stand out before you
You must seek wisdom and knowledge
There are seven elders to watch after you and guide you"

And then Gabriel touched my soul
With a golden hand
Knowledge was imported to me so that I might know
Where it is that I stand

I leaped for joy and almost fell off the couch. I thought what a tremendous thing that has happened? Why should God touch me with such an outpouring of wisdom and love? This was a much more exuberant answer than I expected. Does he have a purpose in mind for me? I sat back down and I kept watching this vision. This was all very exciting.

I felt that I was filled with great Godly love and a joy I had not known before. I saw the history of the world pass before me from the beginning. This went by me so quickly I could only see bits and pieces of what was like a picture show. I saw the flood with Noah. I saw Abraham and his leaving the city to start a new life. I saw the life of Jesus and his ascension which was like a very fast picture show in forward mode. There were many ancient wars. I saw Moses and the parting of water. I saw some of the future and the return of Christ. I saw so many things and it all went by so quickly I could not hope to remember all of it. I then saw the beginning and end of the universe. I did not really understand all that I saw. I thought that time must only exist in the world of lost souls. I mean those who had not reached out to God. Perhaps it is their prison.

> And when the Lord departed
> A rainbow of Love was parted
> A halo of colors stood before me
> So when I looked to heaven, the halo I would see
> And my compassion was great
> I was saved! It was not too late!
>
> I must seek and seek I would
> I must believe and believe now I could

After the vision came to an end, I got out the Bible and read the Gospel of Mark with a new love in my heart for God. It was as if I saw with the eyes of Jesus or with a refreshed perspective. I mean Jesus was trying to show people the way to heaven and eternal life. He said it so many different ways and this is recorded in the Bible, much of it is. They just did not seem to understand him.

> We are but babies in the cradle of the earth
>> Those who do not know, their souls are kept
>> Those who are saved, their souls transgress
> Those who side with evil with Satan are lost
>> As the strong and durable shoots of wheat survive
>> So will the souls that are open and alive

The following days, I was so elated to realize that I knew so much more about heaven than many other people. I became very excited and wanted to immediately tell everyone all about this. I thought they needed to know these things. I wanted to show them how they could get to heaven and have an eternal happy life. I really bounced on everyone with great exuberance with all that I had just learned. Sadly, I found some bitterness about God, disbelief and closed minds. I heard many say that God is dead or, if there is a God, then why do so many terrible things happen. Some said they lost a loved one and they thought God should have not let that happen. After hearing all this negative thinking about God, my faith in God began to sink again. Then I thought that I did not understand the love that had come from God. I became isolated from God again for a short time. I was angry and I did not know why. I became worried, sick and I could not sleep. It was as if Satan tortured me with visions of fear. Why were so many terrible things happening in the world? Why was God letting this happen? It did not seem to me that God was very kind to people. I wanted to withdraw and not reach out. Then I thought my thinking is all wrong. I must be more positive and so I decided to face the world with a new stronger attitude.

A week later as I went to sleep one evening, I asked in prayer why I couldn't get across to people to show them the answer. Why does God let terrible things happen in the world? I prayed with love back into my heart and asked God what were some of the answers? A spirit appeared before me. One of the seven guardians, I presume. I had seen him in the vision from Archangel Gabriel. He said, "Before you can help others you must first cast the demons from your own soul. Seek this!" I then tried to understand what the demons in my soul were that I must cast out. How would I do this? I kept an open mind. Within my thoughts I forgave everyone for their indifference. I asked another religious person I knew for the answer. God must have told him to tell me that I can hate as well. I understood that if I hate or I am angry this allows Satan to entered my soul and torture me.

Later, I went to the gymnasium at work to exercise. As I was dressing in the men's locker room, a military friend and I discussed the pleasure in getting away from the office. He said, "This helps one to relax. When I go to bed in the evening with a problem on my mind, I wake in the morning all happy with the solution." I said, "I was just working on a problem last night."

I returned to the office at work with refreshed ideas. I had new feelings that I could seek out what is faith and what is God's purpose? I told a friend what had happened to me. He gave me a small book to read. It was about the spiritual life of John Bunyan. His book "The Pilgrim's Progress" was published in 1678. He explained this problem such that it might help me. I spent most of the evening absorbed in the meaning of this book. I believed all of it as it was so similar to my experiences. I figured out that this guy had the same problem I had. He took years to figure this out. This was a much longer time period than it would take me with the help of this book. I gained his insight. By the time I reached page sixty-nine, I knew how to cast the devil from my heart. Immediately, I felt good again and my appetite returned. That evening I discovered a new understanding of others mental anguish. I must learn to love everyone in spite of their criticisms and negative thoughts about God. That is, I must have a Christian love and compassion. I will always need to be able to deal with the negative thoughts of others. I must not let that sway me from a loving attitude towards others.

I began to think again about making more friends. I prayed to God that I would like to have a girl friend who loved me. I wanted her to eventually tell me from her heart that she loved me. I wanted my art teacher to help me study art more one on one. I asked her and then she did show me more closely how to improve my art.

That evening as I sat relaxing on the couch, it seemed like the devil was sneaking up to me again. It was as if there were demons all about trying to take me away from God. They wanted to rob this new found Christian love I had found. The demons are nothing but thieves. They touched my spine, or so it felt, with hate and fear. I protested intensely. I renewed my faith and kept my Christian love. I got out the Bible and read the Gospel of John. My eyes were open to where I had been lost.

As I prayed to God, amazingly the rainbow of love came out from heaven again. The Archangel Gabriel came to me floating within a cloud. He held his arms out and said:

> "The devil too is not just an angel but an archangel
> Therefore he is many times more powerful than you realize
> If you side with God, then the devil will be trampled under your feet
> Before God you must be humble
> Then away will go the trouble
> You must continually ask God what to do.
> And then you have found heaven and eternal life."

I understood this to mean that in my life there must be many prayers to God. I must be Christ like and keep the evil away from me by having a strong faith in God.

> *Author's note: I would like to point out that the Archangel Gabriel looks nothing like all the paintings and sculptures I have found. He has long flowing reddish brown hair. He has large eyes, a long straight nose and a large mouth with rather thick but not excessively thick lips. He always has this pinkish red scarf around his neck which is about ten feet long*

and twelve inches wide. He most often wears a dark brown robe with a yellowish rope belt. His sandals are dark brown. He does not have an internal glow like the other angels but his glow comes from behind with golden rays from behind his head. He always seems to have a slight smile on his face and lips. If the Archangel Gabriel were a person living in this time period he would be like the rugged outdoors type or an individualist. This is how I saw him.

That evening as I lie down to sleep
Before God I bowed to his feet
I prayed with all my heart and soul to keep
The devil and all his demons away from my soul
To God I asked this so that I might know
That my heart would be bound to heaven to go

Oh, the devil he tempted me
But he was lacking a heart you see
With a heart that is good and full of love
Satan can only be faking such as from above

Visions of fear flowed to pass
Visions of power if I would ask
I would sit at the devils side
If in him I would abide

Away from me Satan! Go to your murky depths
I can see all you offer is a thousand deaths
I place my faith in God
      To his trust I give my sincerest love
I want peace and harmony with God
      So my soul is sure to go to heaven above

Then in my deep prayers for conviction in Christ and God, what should appear to me but the heavenly hosts in a new vision. I could see Jesus, Abraham, Noah, Moses and Elijah beckoning to me.

And then I yearned in my soul to know
That I desired God at my side, to abide
The Devil I must cast away from me, I can see

I can see Jesus at my side, I see inside
And can that be Moses above me
Behind me I also sense, Elijah with a glow
To my left Abraham and others

And Jesus said, "It is good"
And Moses said, "You have done well"
And the others said, "We are pleased with you"

Then I asked my Lord God to forgive my sins
Jesus laid his hand to my right cheek
      My soul was cleansed
      A stronger feeling of love I have not known

Jesus then grasped my right shoulder with
His left hand and said,
      "This is a reminder this day
      That you not go astray
      And with my hand I will guide you
      To help others know what you do.
      Forget me not!"

From then on the devil was remote from me
Oh, he comes back a little now and then I can see
But then I feel the hand and my memory comes to me
And now I must search, to find out what I am to be

Then Noah showed the flood to remind me
That they too had forgotten and met the wrath of God

Then Moses showed me his discussions with God
And how when he returned to the people they too had forgotten
But he also showed that faith can part water

Moses said,

      "You must have great faith
      You must fly with the angels
      You must love God with all your heart
      Now go and seek this!"

From that time on I remember

      The multi-colored halo
      The touch of Jesus and the purification
      The guiding hand on my shoulder
      The children of Moses who forgot
      What great faith can do!

From that time on

      I can see into heaven more clearly every day
      As my faith strengthens so does my love
      For God and all his children

    I now sense that my guardian, my spiritual mother
    Is an angel with golden hair like no other?
    She constantly beckons me to her side
    I sense her love for me as she is with me, she is beside
    I know that her name is Marianne

    She is a guardian angel that protects me
    I can make my way through life with thee
    I feel more confident about my place with God
    Love is the answer, Satan be gone do not anyone rob
    I am saved and now I must get on with my life.

MY VISION OF THE ARCHANGEL JOPHIEL (JOEL)

April, 1973

I wrote the full version of this vision years later on March 28, 1986 from many loose notes that I recorded soon after the vision in April, 1973. As I pieced together the chronology of the vision God opened up my mind and I recalled more of this fantastic vision. That enabled me to fill in the gaps missing from the loose notes. This vision occurred a month after the first visit from Archangel Gabriel. I had a second fantastic vision where the Archangel Jophiel appeared. The name given to me was the Archangel Joel or the Archangel Jophiel and I could not be sure what the correct name was as they sounded so similar.

I was sitting on the couch listening to music and studying the Bible. I was thinking while reading, "God, let me tell you the story of the Christ in my heart. I emptied my heart for all his love and now it overflows with love. My loneliness gave way to caring for others. My fear gave way to faith and strength from God. I, who am a simple and mortal being, wandered in loneliness and darkness in the later days of my childhood. I can remember when I was a young child I did not trust most persons except my parents. I cared a lot about nature and the noises and scents of the outdoors. I could hear the whisper of the wind and rustling of the leaves in the trees in the forest in my back yard. This was my inner peace and strength. I could sense permanence and strength in these miracles of nature. But, I felt like a feather in the river of humanity. I could not be an individual with inner strength from other people. I just did not want to be close to any one person as I was sure they would only use my good intention for their benefit. This had happened to me several times when I was a teenager and a younger adult."

My thoughts continued, "I have been very unhappy many years. Life for me has been a hell of hells beyond torment that I cannot describe. Many a night I would sit alone and wonder what was I to do about this. I could not figure out why I was so depressed and unhappy. I knew I had a loving mother with whom I could do no wrong. I had done wrong by her many times in the past when I was a child. I had a step-father who was a new father to learn to get along with. I was not sure if he cared about me but it appeared to me he did. This was shown to me by his doing his best to take care of me and my brother Terry. I had just graduated from an engineering college at the University of Missouri at Rolla, Rolla, Missouri and I was offered a job with the government which I took. I lived alone in an apartment nearby my work place. My family lived several states away. My body felt it hurt so much that I took to drinking beer occasionally to numb my senses."

Again my thoughts were, "I was a miserable person. I needed something to fill the emptiness in me. I went to church and made some attempts at making friends. It seems I only alienated some people about me although I did not know why. I took up being a scoutmaster for over 30 boys. This was enjoyable. Some boys were bad and disrupted the whole troop. I ran some of them off so I could reach the other boys. I took these other boys on many camping trips. They all thought the world of me it seemed. I did my best to teach them the ways of the outdoors I had learned as a child. I cared about the seasons in the woods and the plants and animals in the wild. They were my friends. They were predictable and trusting."

I was thinking, "All the time I went to church prior to my vision of being saved, I never really deep down inside heard our Lord God. He was like all the people about me, separate and far away from my feelings. Why would he want me? It seemed I was isolated from people. But, even though I could not seem to open up my feelings to other people, my feelings felt open to the wind, the sun and running stream. The rustling leaves of autumn trees were a symphony to my soul. The bubbling sounds of stream water rushing over worn rocks were a lullaby to my ears and I could sleep deep and soundly to its music. The chirping of birds at play touched my strings of joy and would always bring a smile to my face. This seemed natural to me and I could relate to the wildlife about me."

I continued thinking, "Later, there came a point in my life where it seemed as if all the walls were closing in on me so that I could not even find serenity even in nature. It was as if a life force from within me was dying and yet was also crying to be released, to be free. I was at my apartment, alone, and there was no one to reach out to. Oh, I talked to a number of men and women there at the apartment complex in Huber Heights but they were not really friends. There was no one nearby who cared about how I felt. I felt as if I would wither away and die if I could not open up with my feelings to someone. Last month I had asked God whether I could know more about the struggle with good and evil. I wanted to know what God's plans were for those in the world.

There I sat on the couch staring at the wall in desperation. I thought at this point that my life was lost. Even though I had seen the vision where I had been saved, it did not really sink in, the meaning, that is. There was no one to care for and no one to care for me. I cried out to God, "I believe in Jesus as my savior and I accept him into my heart. God, if you truly exist in heaven above then my life, body and soul are yours to do with as you please. I will be your servant and do your bidding from this time and ever after. Can I be happy? Can you lift the veil from my mind and show me what life is? Is there knowledge in heaven above that I can find, and what of the universe? What is it made of? God I want to talk to you about these things."

Before doubt could interrupt this release of my thoughts and feelings, a miracle did happen. I will explain it as well as I can remember. All those images remain vivid in my mind even years after of writing these words. A very large bright star did appear to me as it was no more than fifty feet away. It came down from a distance and floated there in front of me. It was a warm, silver white on a blue background and it seemed to light up my vision, heart and mind with an uplifting grace. It seemed the other wall of the apartment was no longer there as these visions were coming right through this wall.

From the star overhead there was a cylinder shaped deep blue shaft of light that erupted. At the same instant, a deep humble, but strong voice said to me, "As surely as you have asked, I have a message from your Lord and Savoir Jesus Christ with this light to guide your way. Your soul has been saved by him for our Lord God." The Archangel Jophiel did appear from the star and followed the blue shaft of light towards me. The Archangel Jophiel did summon up two lesser angels that appeared as young persons, one with golden hair and the other with dark red curly locks. Slung about their right shoulders were white cords attached to straight golden trumpets with a mouthpiece at one end and a horn at the other end. Upon command by Jophiel, the lesser angels faced each other and blew heavenly music that penetrated through my very body and soul. I could then feel the pain and desperation leave my body. It was as if there were demons within my body and they could no longer stand to be within me. The horns chased them away from me. Those angelic horns were very soothing. They filled me with joy.

The dark spirits that left my soul cried in anguish as if they were denied their life's blood. The void in my soul was replaced with great joy and happiness. And, as the trumpets blasted away it seemed that the entire universe was shifted by this great force. I sensed that the sun pulsed forth at this instant with great jets of energy. At this time, the Archangel Jophiel did undo a scroll of sacred writings from what appeared as spools of wood with handles. The Archangel Jophiel had long golden hair that flowed about his shoulders and wings. Each wing on either side of his body actually was in three parts and the angel had on a silver-like white flowing robe that went to his ankles, not covering his feet and ankles. At the wrists and ankles the robe had intricate embroidery of golden interspaced rectangular patterns. About the archangel's head was a glow of yellow gold signifying its essence or its life force. It was a strong bright glow. Above the angel's wings it appeared like the glow of burning flames.

At the time of the reading of the scroll a rainbow did appear over and behind the angels with the trumpets as a sign of the promise between me and my Lord. The Archangel Jophiel read the scroll and two other archangels appeared. They were Archangels Michael and Raphael. I could recognize the Archangel Michael by his golden helmet with golden armor. I could tell it was the Archangel Raphael because one of the lesser angels introduced him. Actually they introduced both archangels.

They told me that God speaks of my promise of faith in God. They said that God is very pleased to know a person who is so committed to him with all his body and soul. God was so pleased they said that he decided he would have a special task for me to complete here in this world and then later in heaven as well.

The Archangel Jophiel had a message for mankind from the scroll which he unrolled and with great sincerity he read the following:

> "For I say unto you those who do not accept Christ
> as your savior and redeemer, your sins will fill unto
> you as water pours into a cup. Your cup will be filled
> with sins and being faithless there will be no way to
> empty your cup. When your cup of sins overflows;

your soul will be lost. The devil will see that your cup overflows. He will delight in your misfortune and drink of your cup. The devil will drink and consume your soul. He will rejoice that you are lost. Being lost, the devil will lead you astray even more so you cannot find the path back to God so easily. Oh you poor souls who do not accept Christ as your savior; be it known that in all your days you shall know only days filled with torment.

And, when you are no longer sensitive to your sins and to the hurt you inflict to others, your cup of sin will overflow onto others. The sea of anger and hate that flows from it and on to others will burn their souls. And should you take delight in the sea of torment and hate you have generated, which will overflow from your cup, you will become evil and lost. Then I say to you that the devil is your redeemer (deliverer.) The devil has your soul in his grip.

Oh I say to you who is the maker of torment for the innocent and flock of Christ, your soul will be consumed on your day of judgment. Whether that judgment day is before death or after death, only God can choose. Should it be after death your punishment will be increased one thousand fold. It will be so difficult to find the good souls and heaven. Your struggles will be great at that time. Should judgment day be before death, God has given you another chance to empty your cup and find good. Follow these steps to accept our Lord into your soul.

1. Accept now the sinner that you are for every person has sins.
2. Accept godliness over the delight of sins.

3. Accept happiness over the ecstasy in hurting others.
4. Accept love of all persons and God over hate.
5. Accept your brothers and sisters in God over empty companions who lead you astray.
6. Accept the bridge to eternal life and not the road to death in sin.

And there will be those who live their life in fear of God that their cup may soon overflow. They will constantly look into themselves with the selfish fear of what they might lose. Those people will see when their cup begins to reach the brim. They notice it will begin to overflow if they do not do something soon. They will quickly run to God and pour the top half of their cup of sins over to him.

They do not ask God to be their redeemer, but they only take their sins to God to be seen and heard by him so they hope that they will not be punished. Their hearts are not open to Christ and their eyes only see what is to fear. Face unto me you weak and fearful sinners. Empty your cup of sins and your soul with sins, that Christ may take this away and fill your cup with love."

The lesser angels who held the trumpets said, "Remember these words and write them down for the world to know about good and evil. God will save those who ask to be with our Lord."

The vision then ended when the angels no longer spoke. Shortly thereafter they were all gone.

The Star Announcing the Visit by the Archangel Jophiel

The Archangel Jophiel Reads the Scroll to Me.

CHAPTER SIX

THE RAINBOW OF LOVE AND A PROMISE OF SALVATION AS SPOKEN BY THE ARCHANGEL GABRIEL

April, 1973

My steps to the Great White Throne occurred in separate fantastic visions in the order written in this book. The vision was all in the same evening but it came as separate episodes so to speak. This vision was so complicated and I had only my loose notes for reference. I have done my best to recreate the entire visions as they happened that evening. The angels opened my mind to remember all this once again in thorough detail. I believe now this is a fairly accurate representation of these visions as they occurred to me. You may worry that the details of these episodes will be so vague in my mind that they not are accurate. You might also worry that Satan is influencing what I write down. I am not concerned about this because this vision is strong in my mind. I've thought of it very often. In fact, it has taken me years to sort out all of this so that I could better record it as so much did happen. I wrote a complete narrative of this vision later on October 18, 1987 from many loose notes that were recorded soon after the vision in April, 1973. As I pieced together the chronology of the vision God opened up my mind and I recalled more of this fantastic vision. That enabled me to fill in the gaps missing from the loose notes.

As I sat on the living room couch in my apartment in Huber Heights, Ohio I was in great distress. I was thinking of a way out of all my problems so my mind seemed much troubled at this time. Evil spirits and maybe demons had been following me affecting my health and mental well being. I had recently realized that being saved does not automatically give me inner peace or keep all the demons away. I began to realize that if I was to ever be healthy again, I'd have to cast out away from me all these evil spirits. After much study and thought, I decided that the best way to do this would be again to call on a higher power for help.

Thus, I prayed sincerely to God that he help me cast away these evil spirits and demons. I promised God that I would do for him as he wanted and that I completely trusted him to protect me.

> *Author's Note: I did not know it at that time, but I was carrying an internal infection on my colon that caused me to be sick often and to feel depressed. I was listening to my stereo music to calm myself.*

Things were so bad it seemed to me at that time that I thought that I might as well be dead. I was unhappy with the way things were at my work and I was feeling ill every day. Then I thought back to those times before when the angels came to me and all the promises that they made to me. I thought, "Why was it all so bad now?" Then I cried all the way up to heaven, "God take me; I am no good for anyone here anyway. God save me from evil and illness and show me what life is all about. I totally submit to your will."

What do you think happened? To my surprise God answered me. From out of heaven came a fantastic rainbow that seemed like eternal love. This changed my depression immediately. It was directly in front of me in the living room, but behind it stretching out for what looked to be a great distance were all types of heavenly persons. It seemed to me that thousands of heavenly voices were singing out, "Hallelujah! Praise the Lord! Hallelujah! We love thee!" Above the rainbow I saw a host of many angels. From each side were angels with white robes, curly golden hair and rosy complexions. The rainbow contained all of the colors one would expect to find in an earthly rainbow. It appeared to be about twelve feet in front of me and was twelve feet wide by twelve feet high. The living room wall was no longer visible and heaven appeared to be behind this glowing rainbow.

What should appear next but an angel at each side of the rainbow with long five foot golden trumpets. They blew the instruments with much sound as they were at each side and looking upward at each other. The music was so exhilarating, the hairs rose on my back and I felt light-headed. There appeared a bright glowing golden light at the top which was blinding to behold. As the heavenly golden light subsided, a magnificent angel was facing me.

Then it seemed that many thousands of heavenly voices sang out,

> "Glory to the Lord in the Highest!
> Praise be to our Father!
> Hallelujah! Hallelujah!
> Let all heaven and earth praise the glory of God!"

This angel had a warm friendly smile and intense brown eyes and golden brown long flowing hair. He wore a medium brown robe that was a coarse looking fabric. Under this robe gathered around his neck was a light pinkish-red scarf like adornment. He had a dark complexion and thick lips (not too thick) and large round cheeks. His nose was longer than most and straight. He had a wonderful smile all over his face.

He shouted out,

"Greetings! You are indeed a most blessed person to receive such a welcome. I bring Good News. I am Gabriel, the archangel with the Good News that you seek. May the rainbow of love shower its kindness and richness on you. Heaven opens its doors for your salvation. You are the one we wait for to tell the world that our Lord Jesus, the beloved, is on his way. He will gather his flock and smite the wolves that seek to destroy his sheep."

Then it seemed that many thousands of angels and heavenly persons in heaven sang out most joyously,

"He will triumph!
Our Lord will come!
He is most merciful.
His love knows no bounds!
It is as infinite as the universe!
Prepare the way!"

Then the Archangel Gabriel looked straight at me, opened his arms, held them up and said,

"You have already been saved,
but there is more for you to do!
Come let me show you the way.
Seek and you shall find.
Fear not. God loves you."

He raised his arms and said,

"Behold, the trumpets announce to you the Good News."

Then many angels came up above the rainbow and played beautiful music that gave me a great feeling of ease and love. He raised his arms up again and said,

"Behold, the babies of paradise are happy for you."

I could see many small babies laughing and darting about. They were very happy and played with each other. They had all different hair colors that were red, brown, white and gold. They had small wings at their shoulder blades. Then the Archangel Gabriel raised his arms again and said,

> "Behold, here are the seven who will look after you now.
> They will follow you to tell the world of the coming
> of our Lord Jesus."

I could see seven adults rise above the rainbow. They all had grayish white beards and some had hair on their heads that was as white as snow. They shouted,

> "Hallelujah! Praise the Lord! We love you!
> Listen to us and we will guide you.
> Always seek good and follow the spirit.
> Do not listen to Satan; he will try to destroy you."

Then a majestic golden glow surrounded the Archangel Gabriel and he moved upward another twelve feet.

A highway that looked like blue, red, green and yellow stardust appeared from the distance, curved about and shot over the rainbow and then over my head. I could hear the sound of many thundering horses' hooves pounding and chariot wheels turning. What appeared next but chariots coming out of the highway of star dust. Each chariot was pulled by two heavily muscled horses. Each pair of horses was colored as was the stardust. They pulled chariots that were ornate with red, black, brown and silver ornamentation. A great warrior with golden armor and helmets was in each chariot. I could hear them urging their horses onward. They came at me and over me. There were twelve chariots in all. Then they disappeared behind me. This was very awe inspiring.

The Stairway to Heaven

Just as I thought I could see nothing more colorful and fantastic, an even greater event happened. I could hear the sound of many trumpets and the Archangel Gabriel moved his left hand and arm over to my right.

He said, "Behold the stairway to heaven. Come to me. We need you."

I could see a white stairway unfold from heaven towards me. From heaven it curved to the left, then to the right as it lowered towards me and it curved back again to the left. It appeared like white marble steps the height of any stairway of this type. Underneath it was white and smooth and there was no visible means of its support. It just dropped in front of me seemingly from the sky. Following this again were a series of colored horses and an army of chariots from heaven. They came over the rainbow passed my left and they disappeared in the distance behind me. This was a stairway of white that descended from heaven. There were heavenly persons standing at the first landing summoning me up past the right of the rainbow. They were about 20 feet above me. I looked upward even higher and I could see Abraham who stood much higher upward on the platform above the second landing. He was about 50 feet above me. There were two small landings and one larger landing higher up that was more like the top of the stairs than a landing. This is where Abraham stood.

I remembered that this man opened his arms outward and upward and said boldly, "Behold my seed!" He was tall and had a long white and black beard. I intuitively knew he was Abraham, the father of the Israelites. The angels who were standing at my level told me several times to later write all this down for the benefit of others to know about God and heaven for what I am about to see and receive.

I looked up and on the first landing that was about twenty feet up and there stood a man. He had on a light brown light weight fabric robe with a golden rope belt and he wore brown sandals. His hair was long black, gray and white. He had a long black and gray beard. He had a very intense look in his face and he beckoned to me, "Come to me, my son." He held a great wooden staff in his left hand which had mounted at its top about nine feet up a golden cobra's head with red gemstones for eyes. He raised it up and down twice and said, "You shall look upon my staff and behold the serpent. Do not be afraid. What will you do?" I said, "I will look upon the serpent and remember that my Lord will not let harm befall me." He said, "Very good my son, you have faith. Faith conquers all. Do you know who I am? I am Moses. I took my children out of Egypt across the great sea. God gave me the strength to lead my children to the Promised Land."

Moses continued, "Regrettably they lost their faith. Only a few stayed with God. Satan devoured thousands of them with his stinging tongue. My thoughts were then to write down these events for all the future generations so they could also have the chance to walk across the great sea and find the Promised Land. So I spent my final days, months and years writing all that happened. Do you know why the staff of Satan looks so attractive? He promises many wonderful things. My staff looks fearful, but I do not promise many good things. Only God can promise this. You must have great faith. With God all things are possible. Faith will keep you with God and many blessings will be found. Satan's promises are only tricks so he may destroy your soul. He will promise you wealth and power. What good does it do you to gain the whole world, but lose your soul? When you are here you will not seek earthly things. Wealth and power are but earthly illusions. We have brought you here so you may understand this, defeat Satan and lead our new children to the Promised Land." He spoke very slowly and hesitated often as if asking God for his next words. I believe Moses resembled Peter Falk, the actor, in physical appearance when he was middle aged. His speech and mannerisms were also very similar, but Moses was taller by about six inches than Peter Falk.

Moses talked to me more, "Come to me my son." I walked up the stairs and stood one step below him. He put his right hand on my left shoulder and looked at me intensely with deep dark brown eyes and said, "The books were my greatest accomplishment. They have remained unmolested so they may be as the beacon light of a heavenly lighthouse showing the way to the Promised Land." I grabbed each of Moses' forearms and said, "You are indeed a great man and unselfish. Your wisdom is great."

Another man was at Moses' right side and he just stood there. I did not realize it at that time but it was my spirit body that stood below Moses and not my earthly body. The new person who arrived was a lean, muscular and very attractive. He had curly reddish brown hair and stood about six inches taller than Moses. He looked at me and it seemed that he nearly cried, "I am King David. I have sinned greatly, but God in his infinite kindness and mercy brought me to this place to reign forever as a king. I seek not a kingdom of land, of cities or gold, but I seek a Kingdom of God with all my children happy and loving one another. Once I had a kingdom of great wealth, but here I have treasures beyond any wealth. Remember this. We are all a king of our own souls and we may do with it as we like. God cannot take our soul. Satan cannot take it either. We can, however, give our soul to God or to Satan. I am so happy that you have chosen to give your soul to God. God will take your soul and hold it to his breast with much love and concern for you." David embraced me and cried, "I am so happy for you."

> *Author's note: This is a very important fact to remember. We are king of our own souls and we may do with it as we like. God or Satan cannot take it from us. Satan may try to trick us into giving it to him, but God will not. God will use only love to guide us to our salvation. We can give our soul either to God or Satan. What will be your choice?*

Another man was to King David's right side and he stood there while King David talked. He was much shorter and had curly black hair and a curly black beard that was down to his chest. He wore an animal skin that covered all but his arms shoulders and legs. He had hairy arms and legs. He had leather sandals and held a short crooked staff in his left hand. That staff looked like a tree branch he had just picked up. From his waist there was a rope belt which also held a leather pouch that hung below it. He reached into this pouch and took out all his treasures. He said, "I would gladly give you all that I have to go back with you and teach my children. They do need the light. They live in a world of darkness. Why must they always harm themselves and others? They are like children who need a teacher to protect them."

I said, "Are you the prophet, Elijah?" He stepped back and was greatly surprised. He said, "The angels have indeed chosen well. Yes, I am the wanderer of the deserts. I wandered and looked into the wilderness for years for my Lord. But I found him not in the wilderness, but in my heart. I see you have also found our Lord in your heart. Treasure this well. Bring us others to love. I am, yes I am Elijah, the prophet. I am here to welcome you to that which you seek."

I had just seen and been with Moses, King David and Elijah. I was very elated! I considered this a very humble event and I felt much honored to be with them and receive their guidance and wisdom. I looked up to the platform above the second landing up much higher and I could see a very tall muscular man with a long white robe held by a golden cord about his waist. He had a long silver white and black beard that came down upon his chest. The hair on his head was also the same colors and was very long over his shoulders. He held the hand of a shorter woman with jet black hair and she wore a dark green dress with a yellow vest and a yellow cord about her waist.

He looked at me and others below and said, "I am that I am. I am Abraham." He looked down to all four of us and again said boldly, "Behold! My Seed! What will you do now?" They all looked at me and I said probably the most important words in my life, "I will love my Father with all my heart, body and soul. Let me be with all of you always. I wish to heal the wounded hearts of those who hurt and are in pain. Lord. I am in pain also. My life is not what I want and I am not at all well. I am greatly distressed. My chest feels like there is a great wound and blood is flowing from me. Will you give me strength? Without you, Lord I am nothing. I promise to follow you all my life as long as I shall live." Abraham resembled Sean Connery the actor in looks and voice. Then I knelt down in front of Moses, King David and Elijah and said, "I pray for all those whom you seek. Let me be your staff. Wield me, hold me, take me, I will yield to you. May I reach but one other person and my life is worth while. Lord, it is my desire to reach but one other person!" Abraham said, "So be it. In you I am well pleased." Then he raised his right hand high above his head and I could see that he also had a great staff in his left hand. Behind him were many of his friends and family. They all seemed to be very happy.

The Heavenly Battle for My Soul

Next, I walked back down the heavenly stairs to my apartment floor. What appeared next above me to my left was a great horse thundering towards me. On this blue horse was a warrior with a blue shield. He said, "We are the horsemen that patrol the earth day and night to keep it safe and tell God of these things which he must know." This horse thundered to me and then turned to my left. Another horse then came from heaven and was bright red. On it was a warrior with a red shield. He carried a lance. He came at me then turned to my right. A gray horse with black spots came from my right and was moving to my left. He pulled a stretcher hooked to the saddle with two poles where the ends dragged on the ground. In it was a woman with two babies in her arms. She cried with much grief and said, "For all those who have fallen in battle I grieve." A warrior with bandages around his head and left shoulder held the reins of the horse and walked along the side of the horse left on my side. I could see he was in much pain. He said, "Woe is me, why does the world seek to kill me?" He disappeared to my left. Behind him were many women crying and lamenting. "Our sons have died, where are our children?"

When they were gone another great white horse came to me. On it was the greatest warrior. He had golden breast plate and helmet with a crown of feathers. He carried a golden lance in his left hand, held the reins with his right hand. He held a double edged sword in his teeth. He proclaimed boldly, "I will strike down those who murder. The Lord will have justice." He rode towards me, pulled back on the reins and his white stallion reared up on its rear legs. He dismounted his horse and walked over to me. He gently placed his right arm around my upper back for he was taller. Although he did not say who he was, I know this was the Archangel Michael for he was introduced to me in the previous vision a few weeks ago. He said, "I and my warriors will protect you. You need not worry about the demons. We will slay them as we have in the past. He asked one of the lesser angels to get me a stool to sit down upon. Then two lesser angels brought forward a very ornate stool with an ivory white cushion and golden threads sewn into the fabric creating an elaborate pattern. The four legs of the stool were of an ornate Queen Anne style and were golden color. I did sit down on the stool. The warrior said we have placed a rope barrier in front of you so that no demon may harm you. The barrier was a golden rope about one inch in diameter. It was strung from one upright post to another for a span of over 20 feet.

Then the great warrior mounted his white horse and took the sword from his teeth and swung it around in circles with his right hand above his head. He shouted loudly, "Let the battle begin!" I could not imagine what was happening. I heard roars to my right and looked over to see many hideous demons and serpents coming at us so that it appeared the battle would take place in my living room. The warrior headed straight at them and threw his lance to them. It was like a bolt of lightning and one lance killed numerous demons. Next, I heard many horses and chariots coming from my upper left at a very fast pace to face the demons in battle. They were happy. They all shouted, "Long live the prophet! Kill the demons!" The angels rode into the hundreds of demons. All the angels, but the Archangel Michael was slain so that only demons were left. Some demons were on foot and others were riding hideous looking beasts.

The Archangel Michael was still upright on his stallion. After this, a second wave of chariots with foot soldiers that carried large shields and lances came. As they walked toward the demons and the battle that would happen soon, I could hear the rhythm of the cadence of their footsteps. The Archangel Michael yelled in a very high pitched voice, "Slay the evil ones!" I heard trumpets playing marching tunes. There was another battle and they slayed many more demons and drove other demons back until they fled for their lives. The great warrior on the white stallion came back to me. His horse reared up again and he held the head of a demon in his right hand. He shouted out, "Because you had great faith we triumphed!" Then I could see many tired, wounded and dead coming from the battle moving back to my left. I was on the opposite side of my apartment at this time facing where the couch had been. The dead were carried by horses, chariots and soldiers. What a tragedy I thought. A whole battle for my soul, but we won the day. But Satan lives on to come back another day.

Much later it occurred to me that this could have been a replay for my benefit of the great battle in heaven when the Archangel Lucifer and his angels fought the heavenly hosts of God under the Archangel Saint Michael. This, I was not told, but it could be so. Or, it could have been a display of how my faith impacts those in heaven. This I can only wonder about. Even if this was not so, I learned that there are great battles in the spirit world for our souls.

We should pray in reverence for all those who do battle for our souls. Do not lightly take that which is your worth. Each person is worth very much to the heavenly host who fight for them, their faith and then their souls. Be happy for this. Each of us is worth so much to our Lord and his angels that we should take care to be good and serve God.

The Entrance to Heaven

This event ended and I was immediately transported up to the heavenly gates. It happened so quickly that I was not fully aware how I got to this location. I looked up and saw Saint Peter with red brown curly hair and a red curly beard. He was standing in front of two fluted pillars with scrolls of stone draped over their tops. Between the pillars was a gate of gold and pearl. It opened in the middle towards us as Saint Peter took golden keys to them. He said, "I am Saint Peter and I hold the keys to heaven. Enter with love in your heart." As I walked through the gates I shook his hand and thanked him.

Beyond the gate was each of the other 12 disciples that were once with Jesus in Israel. I shook all their hands, but Saint John embraced me and said, "Bless you, my brother." Judas was last. He did not shake my hand. He cried, "I grieve so much. I sold my Lord to the devil for only so much silver. Here is my reward." He held up a rope with a noose in his right hand. "Please forgive me Father" were his words. But Judas then took my right hand and led me to a special room. It was up on a platform and only enclosed by three foot high railings with spindles about the entire room below the hand rails. He said, "I am allowed to lead you to the judgment room, bless you my brother." Then he was gone.

CHAPTER SEVEN

THE JUDGMENT ROOM AND THE GOLDEN HALLS OF RECORDS

April, 1973

The vision from the previous chapter continued. I wrote a complete narrative of this vision years later on October 18, 1987 from many loose notes that were recorded soon after the vision in April, 1973. As I pieced together the chronology of the vision God opened up my mind and I recalled more of this fantastic vision. That enabled me to fill in the gaps missing from the loose notes.

Judas left me and I walked up four golden steps to a special room. It was two times twenty feet (40 feet) wide to the left by 20 feet deep straight ahead from the stairway entry. As I stood there looking all about I could see that all around this room was a golden railing that was the height of the upper part of my thigh or about 3 feet. The railing was supported by evenly space spindles with elaborate turns that were no more than 12 inches apart. The railing was all around this room that was on a platform above the floor where I met the disciples of Jesus. There was a break in the spindles about three feet wide and 3 steps upward through an opening which I walked through. There was a gate at this opening but an angel held open the gate for me. I stepped up to the room that was on the platform. The floor of this room looked like light colored hardwood. There was another stairway straight ahead across the room. The stairs began inside the room that was up on a platform going above the railing on the other side of this room to an even smaller but similar room that was up higher above my head. It was about 20 feet or more above the room that was a platform. The end of the room was straight ahead from the entrance where I had just climbed the 3 steps.

Straight ahead and a little to the left against the far railing was a long table that was twelve feet long and 12 feet divided by 3 feet (four feet) wide. It sat on the opposite side of the room with the long part of the table parallel to the far railing. On this golden table was a large gold key. Then I looked upward along a stairway that looked like cherry wood steps and marble risers with cherry wood spindles holding a white hand railing on both sides up to the small room 20 feet upward and there I saw an elder with a long white beard and no hair upon his head. The stairway was curved a little to my left then a much greater curve to my right and it appeared to have no visible means of support. This elder who sat at a desk on a high stool that had spindles in the chair back had his feet on the chair foot rest. He wore a very light brown almost off white light fabric robe. The desk looked like a writing table with a sloping surface. He was writing something in a large book on this desk. The elder wore a white flowing robe and held a writing feather in his right hand. On the table was the large book which was opened at the middle. The elder said to me, "I will now write down your name in the *Good Book of Names*. Tell me, can anyone give me any reason that I should not do this?"

From above to my left flew three angels down to the judgment room. They had long golden hair and flowing white robes and wings. As they stood in the judgment room, they held a long scroll unraveling it before us. One angel held each end, the third moved down the scroll pointing his index finger all along it. The scroll was unlike those used by those of my world. The writing was across the ends of the material on which was written many words rather than from the left spool to the right spool. He said with confidence, "We see nothing in here to stop you from writing his name in the *Good Book of Names*. He has been a good, honest person only misguided by the darkness of his world. Go ahead and place his name along with the others in the heavenly place. What will be his place in heaven?" The angels took me by my arms and shoulders and lifted me upward. I could see numerous heavenly places to live, all floating on white clouds. Some were green pastures, some were farms and still others were cities. I could see many happy persons beckoning me to come to their homes in heaven. The Archangel Gabriel appeared before us and said, "No, none of these places will you abide." I was flabbergasted. I said to the angel, "Does this mean I do not get to live in heaven?" He did not answer me but just smiled. Then the angels took me to another great place in heaven.

The Angels Show Me New Jerusalem

What appeared before me next was a great walled fortress. At each corner and spaced at regular intervals were guard towers. The towers were octagon shape. I could see soldiers dressed in black and white with belts that crossed over their chest and shoulders. They were patrolling the walls. They wore tall head dressed type helmets as a part of their uniforms. The left and right sides of the helmets were black with dome shape and a curved shaped white metal tongue like decoration split the helmets from the top to the bottom such that the spoon shaped white metal that curved gracefully upward and was rounded was just above their eyes. The jacket part of their uniforms was black sleeves with a white metal vest. Their black belts at their waists held black and white pleated fabric short dress like uniform. Their black and white sandals had leather straps part way up to their knees.

The walled city was as gold glass. It looked like gold but is was so smooth and shining it appeared as glass. It was miles wide. It sat on a foundation of many gemstones of all colors. In the middle of each wall at each of the four sides was a great high gate. I could only see two gates and they had bars of gold to lock them tight. Medallions of gemstones and pearls were at the middle of the doors. The angels said, "This is New Jerusalem. Presently, no one lives here but the heavenly soldiers' patrolling the walls. This is the promised city for our Jewish children who will be gathered by our Lord." Then Gabriel appeared before us again and said, "You will not abide in this place either." I thought now this makes sense as I am not Jewish. The three angels took me back to the judgment room. As they did I looked over my right shoulder at the beautiful city thinking this would be a wonderful place to live for eternity. It rotated around and around and disappeared into the distance. I could see no one living within.

The Angels Take Me to the Judgment Room and to the Halls of Records

Next, I stood by the table again, but now it was red like rosewood. On the other side of the gold key was a very ornate scale with an all gold circular platform and chains which held the plates for balancing an item to determine its weight. The elder walked down the stairs and stood beside me. He carried a rosewood rectangular box. He opened it and withdrew three small golden weights. Each was a different size and was cylindrical with ball shaped handles on top with which to grasp them. The elder said to me quite frankly, "This is the standard by which we will measure you." He placed the weights into the plate on one side of the scales that was next to us to my right. He then said to the angels, "Bring me the records of this man and we will measure him."

Astonishingly what appeared before us next was a great golden hallway of many thousands of drawers all along each of the walls of the hallways. The two angels took me up again and carried me toward one of the hallways. The third angel flew to and fro all about the walls. It was as high and deep as could be seen by my eyes. I could see other angels all about opening drawers and placing golden sheets therein that looked like index cards. Then we moved downward a great distance and the third angel pointed to a drawer. On it was my name. The third angel beckoned that the drawer be opened. When what should appear but another angel who was a woman with breasts that were covered by an ornate fabric pink breast plate and she had jet black hair and beautiful wings that were pink. She opened the drawer. I could see it was twelve inches wide inside, twelve inches divided by two high (6 inches high) and twelve inches multiplied by two deep or its length (24 inches deep). It was filled with cards that were only in the first six inches of the drawer. The third angel took the golden cards and held them up in front of me. He said, "See the good deeds of your life in my hands. See the drawer. There is room for many more good deeds in this drawer, but we do not want to say that the ones you already have do not have value for they do. We will take these to the Judgment Room."

We flew back to the room again and this time there were many elders and angels in and all about the room. The third angel slowly placed the golden cards that were my life's good deeds on the other plate to my left of the golden scales of justice. They slowly moved the plate downward and the three weights moved upward until the scale pointer was just barely on the side of golden cards. This meant my golden cards outweighed the weights. Another way to say this is that the good in me outweighed the bad in me. All the elders and angels sang out, "Praise the Lord! We have measured you and you are justly judged to be worthy. May God take you forever!" I was so happy I jumped up and down and sang with them and they all laughed happily. What happened next was that I found myself sitting back on my couch in my apartment living room. I was almost in shock for what had just happened.

I was Full of Love and It did Feel Very Good.
By Dennis W. Schroll 1983

My heart feels twisted inside and out
I grieve for you who can't understand
It is so clear what it is all about
The way to reach the Promised Land.

So when you strive for a better life
Remember that in living is loving
And in loving is losing all the strife
Conquer your fears, lose yourself

I lost myself and found you
You want me to be close
You care about me, it is true
Hold me closer, keep me close

I can cry and the pain won't go away
The tears in my eyes let go
Why do you go when I want you to stay?
When in you all my hopes I can see, I know.

You are a delight to behold
When my heart is heavy with grief
I always know you want me to hold
To hold you close you are what I seek.

Oh, bring me down bring me home
My tears are for you who are so good
Can you take me? Don't leave me alone!
I know you will treat me as you should

I don't care about anything at all
As long as I am with you
Everything will be alright, I saw
If I am beside you

I love you; I need you; if you return my love
I know everything will be alright
Alright for you and for me in heaven above
That is all I care about. You are my light.

CHAPTER EIGHT

VISION OF MY VISIT TO THE GREAT WHITE THRONE, PART 1

April, 1973

This vision was a continuation of the vision at the Judgment Room. I wrote a complete narrative of this vision years later on March 28, 1986 from many loose notes that were recorded soon after the vision in May, 1973. As I pieced together the chronology of the vision God opened up my mind and I recalled more of this fantastic vision. That enabled me to fill in the gaps missing from the loose notes.

My visit to the Great White Throne had instilled in me many mixed feelings for years. At times I would doubt it and think my mind had left me. At other times I would believe in it with great faith. With faith so strong, God would send blessings and miracles to me ever more so frequently. Many times God would send an angel or person such as Moses to me in a vision. They were as if real, but they were heavenly, not earthly. They would remind me of my pact with God so how could I doubt my visit with God. Many other times I would look up similar events in the Bible and words of others who had visions. Many aspects of their visions were very similar to my visions so I would see my visions were real. I did this after writing my vision onto paper so I would not contaminate my vision with information from the Bible. I wanted to compare what they saw and experienced with what I experienced. I would find very many similarities to my vision. Their visions were never stated as completely and in as much detail as were mine. That would again kindle my faith that these visions were real. Here now are my visions in as much detail as I can put to paper including much detailed descriptions. I want the reader to experience the full impact of the visions in as much detail as I could recall. Also, I think the reader will more easily believe what I say with more detail.

After visiting the hall of records and the judgment room, what happened next was that I was sitting back on the couch in my living room. This is where I started. I could still see the rainbow of love and the stairway to heaven still in front of me. I was confused. I asked God did he reject me. Then I prayed, "Take me Lord, do not leave me alone."

The next thing that happened was that two angels who had a firm determination in their faces quickly flew down to me. They grabbed me very quickly under my upper arms. They lifted me upward and took me away. As they did I could feel in my stomach a feeling of flight like that one experience when riding on the roller coaster. I looked back over my left shoulder and I could see my body still on the couch. That was a slightly disturbing thought. Was I dead? It occurred to me that when I am in that worldly form on the couch I am greatly limited in my ability to see and understand the universe. I mostly felt burdened there in my worldly body and there was much pain on the earth for me. I had also observed this pain in many others. But up here with the angels I felt very happy. I felt very good. There was no pain. Later, it occurred to me that this is how Adam and Eve must have felt when Eve took the temptation of the apple. They were burdened with earthly pains.

Before I could go on to the Great White Throne, I was tested by the demons and the fires of hell. At the time I did not know that I was to visit the Great White Throne with God.

CHAPTER NINE

I WAS TESTED, THE FIRES BETWEEN HEAVEN AND HELL, PART 2

April, 1973

The vision continued. I wrote a complete narrative of this vision years later on October 18, 1987 from many loose notes that were recorded soon after the vision in May, 1973. As I pieced together the chronology of the vision God opened up my mind and I recalled more of this fantastic vision. That enabled me to fill in the gaps missing from the loose notes.

Prior to my visit to the Great White Throne in 1973, I also experienced another revelation. It was revealed to me how our souls could be passed through the heavenly walls of fire at the edge of hell. The two angels carried my spirit body by my upper arms with an angel on each side of me. They showed to me the following revelation. The angels were aglow with silver white light and had golden curly hair that glowed as gold or the evening sunset. All this was very beautiful to behold.

From a distance I could see a great ball of fire that was very large as is the sun, but it was not the sun. Great anguish and hideous screams emanated from this ball of fire that glowed red everywhere. I was thinking, "Perhaps it was a view of the edge of hell from a great distance." The angels then said, "You will be tested, your time had come to pass. My soul and its worth to God would be passed into the edge of hell through heavenly walls of fire." At that moment a great fear swept over my whole being as I did not know what would happen.

The angels then let go of me and left. I began to fall. A hideous looking dragon swiftly flew upward at me and caught me in its grasp. This dragon was about 40 feet long and had four legs with large claws at the end of four fingers and opposing thumbs on each leg. He was yellowish green with scales and had reddish blue wings at his midsection. His strength was much greater than mine. When he grasped me with his four clawed fingers, my body was paralyzed. He could not be resisted. The dragon which really did look like a dragon of folklore on my world had a long snout like a crocodile with big nostrils that breathed flames and smoke. He looked at me with his large glowing red eyes set into dark eye balls and said, "You are mine. You will be tormented beyond your wildest imagination. You cannot escape. You are lost and given to me." The dragon also had winged gills from behind his snout down to his neck that looked like his wings which were reddish blue. The wings and gills looked like a folding fan or spines with membranes between them. He looked very much like a very large Chinese dragon with wings.

The dragon then turned his head looking forward and he rolled his long forked red tongue out. He let out a piercing scream! He carried me into a wall of fire where I thought I would die. When I passed through and was still alive, I thought my only chance of preventing my demise was to call out for heavenly help. I cried, "Jesus, my Lord, save me from this terrible fate." I felt no pain but after we had burst through this wall of flame another wall of fire could be seen beyond that. Between these two walls could be seen the souls of thousands upon thousands of tormented people's souls. They looked as persons but were distorted spiritual bodies flying all about. They looked to be in a great panic and were filled with terror. They were rapidly flying from one direction to another. They all moved about in a random fashion as if they were trying to escape from a great monster.

In their panic they were trying to get away but they did not know which way to go. They had been tested, but they had not the faith in our Lord. They were quite blind to our Lord so they could not see their fate. They could not see the guiding light of faith. They were in crazed confusion as to their state of affairs. They were lost and they did not know what to do. At a distance I could see, but they could not see, huge demons consuming others like them who were lost souls. To me they looked like they were sheep being led to the slaughter. They were lost souls, and then they were gone. To hell I suspected. The demons trapped their souls and they were lost. At that moment the angels blew trumpets and told me, "You were tested and your faith saved you. Those who were lost had no faith in God and they could not believe they could be saved so they were blind to our Lord. They were in great confusion and torment. They were being taken to the fiery pits where the demons would consume them, for when their judgment came, they had not believed in God. Your faith kept you from the fiery pits and you see the light of God." The angels then took out great silver swords which gleamed of light and slew the dragon. Those with lost souls tried to grab onto me hoping they would be able to escape but the angels threw them off me. One angel said, "You were tested and found lacking. You cannot be saved by this person. Only God can save you." I was so relieved to be saved from this terrible fate.

Again I had prayed to be saved by God and was saved. Two angels carried me in my spirit form again through one wall of fire and away from this awful sight. I remembered that I could see the fiery pit with all sorts of agony and torment experienced by those within. It was as if a lake of fire had red-like blood for water with flames leaping from the surface. Dotted across its surface were small islands on which the spirits and souls of many who had died were crowded trying to escape the flames. The angels who were carrying me said

"See those who attempt to escape the flames. They are doomed. Soon the dragon will devour them and they will be lost. They had not the shield of faith and were weak of faith in God. Satan has taken their souls. They did not ask Jesus to save them and now they will suffer." It was a terrible sight to behold.

> *Author's note: I want to make something perfectly clear here. God did not put these people into these situations. These people had the freedom of choice and they put themselves into these situations. Many were led astray by evil persons. Consider though that each person has free will to choose. Their faith was lacking, but the people that were strong of faith escaped from these evil persons and found their way to good and God. I plead with you that if you are struggling with an evil person, do not let that person confuse you such that you lose your soul. Be brave. They were not brave.*

The angels, one of them on each side of me, again took me by my upper arms and they flew me towards the next wall of fire. This wall of fire was different for it glowed as if holy and did not look as flames like those near hell. They said "Now we will burn away all those things not suited for those who are most holy in heaven. All those evil and worldly things will be burned from you to be left here where they are suitable for this evil place we left." They took me through three walls of these fires and as a bundle of straw my spirit burned until all bad and worldly things passed from me. All that was left was now pure and holy. My spirit now glowed as did the angels and I was most holy. The angels said, "Now you are pure and may be taken to the throne of our Lord."

It was as if we were in the darkness of space and I could see in all directions. In the distance I could see a great blood red lake which had occasional releases of fire upward from its surface. The light was dim but the reflection off the lake made the sky seem light red as well. I could see a small island not too far in the distance and a spirit of a man was struggling to climb out of the lake onto the island. One of the angels said to me, "See how he is struggling on his own with no help from an angel or even a friend. He does not know it now, but Satan has him in his grips and he is a lost soul. The lost souls in the lake of blood of hell are all too occupied with their own agonies. Their only hope is to reach out to our Lord. They have not our Lord's helping hand to pull them from the agonies of hell." Upon looking into hell that day I learned a great lesson. It is our faith in God and concern for others that keeps us on a path to heaven and away from agony and suffering.

CHAPTER TEN

REFLECTION UPON THE WALLS OF FIRE BETWEEN HEAVEN AND HELL, PART 3

March, 2012

Many persons do not realize the precarious situation that we are walking through during our lives. Consider my experience I just related in the previous chapter, the fires between heaven and hell. It would be easy for each and every person to fall into hell with much confusion or to be saved. This is a decision that is up to each and every person. Do not be led about like an animal which has no thought of his own but his or her best interests. Each person must make their own decisions. Now you know that you can be carried by angels to heaven based solely only on your own immediate reaction to these horrifying events. Being prepared even before death is important. Having faith and belief in God prepares one for the events after death where decisions must quickly be made. This could be soon after one's death. Remember to not fear the dragon and evil when you have God on your side. God will save you from all these terrible situations. With our Lord, you need not worry about being confused by Satan. If you are confused then pray and ask God for help. God is always there whether in this world or in the fires between heaven and hell. Without our Lord, one maybe easily led astray or confused by these events. This is especially true if one really had very little familiarity with God all their lives.

So as many godly persons before have said to people in this world be prepared for terrible events that could follow death. To be with our Lord, pray often and have strong faith in God. Why would one save up your money or treasures in this world when you will be here only a short time? It is better to save up those heavenly treasures like love, compassion and grace from God in this world and they will be there upon death. Jesus said something like this two thousand years ago.

This is an experience that I believe all persons must face when they die. I cannot be certain of this but I think people should be prepared for this time which they will face after they pass away. I was taken on the same path, I believe, as that of a deceased person. I was enlightened so that I would know what it will be like after death. God wanted me to know all about this and come back and relate this to all living persons who will listen so they will be prepared for death. I took the path of a deceased person but I had not died. It was as if God raised me back from death to the living as Jesus had once raised Lazarus from death. Many people want to deny that there is even a hell to escape from. Satan clouds their mind with good thoughts so they think they will simply walk into heaven with a deceased family member to guide them. Woe to them who deny the darkness and agony of hell. They may find themselves there without any way to escape. Have faith in God and ask for his help. Do not think you will escape because hell is not real. Woe is to those who are arrogant and deny God.

Later in my studies, I learned the following lessons that many Christians of our past had learned. They had tried to communicate this with their brethren, neighbors and descendants. When we are saved we make contact with God each in our own way. We must learn to have faith, praise our Lord, and pray for good things for ourselves and others here in this world. If we do this it will be there after death. Now that we are of the Church of God we must receive the Holy Spirit and grow strong in our Lord. This means we must not only read the word and speak the word, but we must put on a new attitude and have Christian behavior. In my attempts to bring others to God I learned that we who are saved cannot expect the unsaved and those in need to want to be here in our church unless we put off the old person [Ephesians 4:30-32 *(Put off the old person)*] and put on the new person [Colossians 3:15-17 *(Put on the new person to be in Christ.)*]

Let us pray to Jesus Christ for the souls of the people who are in need.

> "Lord, we must stop thinking of ourselves and all of our problems. We will always have problems. Lord, help us to pray for others and serve God so that we can save others when possible. To save others means we must think of others and be supportive, being there when needed. Many who come to us when at church, at work or anywhere else must see Jesus in us if we do indeed walk in the new person. When we seek those who are in need, we must be ready at anytime! Jesus said that we must help to save the lost sheep (Luke 15:1-7.) Lord, help us to reach out more to others with friendship and love. We must go to the new people in church first, not our friends. The needs of our friends will not always be as great as those who are troubled and seek answers. Those who are unsaved or those who are weak in the faith fall easily if we do not put forth the strong efforts to reach them and be supportive. Lord, we must be there to catch those who begin to fall, and we must be supportive. We must remember God will work through us and he can do his good works more easily if we touch the hearts of others. We must not be overbearing or get frustrated. God help us to walk in Jesus' footsteps and be patient. Patience bears rewards. Praise be it to God and may all of you have great joy! Amen."

CHAPTER ELEVEN

MY VISIT TO THE GREAT WHITE THRONE CONTINUES, PART 4

April, 1973

My visit to the Great White Throne continued after I was taken through the walls of fire between heaven and hell. I wrote a complete narrative of this vision years later on October 18, 1987 from many loose notes that were recorded soon after the vision in May, 1973. As I pieced together the chronology of the vision, God opened up my mind, and I recalled more of this fantastic vision. That enabled me to fill in the gaps missing from the loose notes.

The next thing I knew the angels had carried me to a great glowing place. It glowed with silver white light and with gold radiance. This was all seen as rays radiating all about like the sun. The angels told me they are taking me to a place to prepare me to see God. They said, "God loves you and wants to meet you. He will give you instructions regarding your place in the universe and the world below. God wants you to serve him in the future. You are reminded again to write down all that you see and hear. Later you will be told what is to be done with this writing." I was placed on a pathway within a large forest in the mountains but it was not worldly. In the distance I could see a great mountain. I thought this must be where God dwells.

I could see in the distance great flashes of silver light and I could hear resounding thunder claps. It was like the snow clad summit of a majestic mountain. Suddenly, the two angels set me down on my feet and said, "You have arrived here for judgment! From here you must now go on your own. Your faith and strength of heart must carry you further along this path to the Great White Throne of God!" I could see a long winding white path that was lined with flowers. I thought that this pathway must be going to the summit of that mountain on which God's throne sat. Immediately in front of me was a snow white donkey and all about were white forest animals like rabbits and chipmunks. The angel said, "You may ride the donkey if you please. Our Lord will receive you according to this custom."

I sat on the donkey with both legs to the right side initially, but swung my left leg over the donkey's head to have more stability as the animal began to walk. An elder with no hair on his head except near his ears had a long white beard and a pretty maiden as tall as the shoulder height of the elder with long golden hair stepped over and grabbed the reins of the white donkey. The elder looked at me and the maiden did not, she looked towards God. They both then turned to the mountain and led me that way. I could see clouds with lightning and hear thunder claps on the mountains summit. They said nothing with their backs to me and led me down the path. The path was lined all the way with beautiful trees, flowers and forest animals. The plants and animals right on the edge of the path were white, but the trees, plants and animals further away had color as on earth.

We went along the path until we came to a magnificent water fall that allowed volumes of water to spill out into the lake. The waterfalls were numerous in the locations in which they spilled over into the lake from various heights. There was water falling from a height of over fifty feet and water down lower falling about twenty feet. The water fell into a medium sized placid lake which was still some distance away. When we arrived at the banks of the lake, we stopped there to rest. The elder had a pack slung over his shoulder and he took it off and took what appeared to be a water proof bag out of the pack. He filled it with water from the lake and gave the donkey water by pouring water from the bag into his cupped hands. We were there long enough that the donkey had his fill of water. The maiden said to the elder, "Our Lord awaits us and we should be on our way." We began our journey once again. The trail began to wind more closely about the side of the mountain and it began to get steeper. The donkey did not appear to be getting tired nor did the elder or the maiden. We went along this path until I could see dark clouds all about nearby the mountain summit and also far away from the mountain. There were magnificent lightning bolts in the sky all about the mountain summit.

This pathway seemed to go on for miles to the great thundering mountain summit. The great snow peak was constantly illuminated all about by lightning flashes that were accompanied with loud thundering claps. I could tell we closed our distance to the summit by the louder thunder claps. This miracle only held my attention a short time for the ride on the white donkey seemed so gentle and soothing. The peace that I felt was overwhelming. I mean this relaxed me tremendously. Words do not suffice to describe all the flowers and animals that lined the white winding pathway. They were very plentiful. When the tall elder and fair golden haired maiden led the donkey by the reins, they were so quite; I could not even hear their footsteps. In the distance I could see towering boulders overlooking serene lakes. All about this spectacular scenery were trees of all kinds but mostly they were evergreen trees. There was a gentle breeze that brought the aromatic fragrance of the flowers to my senses. The scent was very delightful. Along the way we passed another large towering waterfall at our left that was at least 50 feet high.

CHAPTER TWELVE

ENTRY TO THE GREAT WHITE THRONE OF GOD, PART 5

April, 1973

The journey along the path continued. I wrote a complete narrative of this vision years later on October 18, 1987 from many loose notes that were recorded soon after the vision in May, 1973.

Next we began a slow trek upward around the side of the towering mountain. The pathway became narrower. Over to my right side was a sheer drop off. I did not worry for I felt quite secure with the gentle donkey and the elder and maiden. We climbed upward around and around the mountain until we reached a plateau just below the snow line. In the distance I could see a large crow and I could hear much talk and laughter. I could see what appeared to be a very large outdoor patio with marble flooring. There were upright columns here and there and a few small white buildings that looked like temples. The buildings had domed roofs and some had pitched roofs. They were all white and gold. There were many columns on these buildings. I could see many children and young men and women run out to happily greet me. What a wonderful surprise it was to see them. Most of the people wore tunics that appeared to be white light weight garments which flowed downward to the middle of their upper legs. They were carrying palm leaves and some played stringed instruments. They played lyres, phorminxs, citharas and pandoris.

> *Author's Note: I had to look up these musical instrument names from my memory of what they looked like.*

We had arrived at the summit of the mountain. All that remained was to climb steps to the very top. There was snow at the exterior of the steps so the steps were the only easy way to climb upward.

As I rode the donkey into the crowd they shouted many greetings as they were very excited to see me. They stood along the path and waved the palm leaves to and fro and the maidens threw flower petals all about in front of me. It was such a thrill to be greeted so warmly and enthusiastically. I did not understand why everyone was so happy to see me. It filled me with happiness though to be thought of in such a kind manner. I could hear songs from stringed instruments and many sang out to me.

> "He has come! He has come!
> We are glad! He has come!
> Bring out the people.
> Show him our flowers.
> Maidens sing out delight.
> We all love his sight.
> For he has come!
>
> Our children are happy.
> We greet you with praise.
> Love! Love! Love! He has come!
> We greet you, our *chosen one*.
> You have come to us. It is done."

As the donkey pulled into the crowd, many more children and young adults came over to greet me. I was bewildered by all this and why they all were calling me the *chosen one*. Clearly they knew some things that I did not know. They lifted me off the donkey and carried me shoulder high over to an elderly man who had a long white beard. Other than his beard, his hair was only around the base of his head. This man sat on a stool at the base of many steps that led upward to where before I could see the lightning flashes and hear thunder. Strangely enough, it was quite now. The man was sitting at a tall desk that supported a large golden bound book. The man waved his hands and shouted, "Be quite now! His Holiness wishes his audience." He looked into his book, found my name, and checked it off as if he were taking my ticket to an auditorium.

Right after he checked off my name, the children sang the same tune as before. But it was in an organized fashion where they stood. Then a children's choir sang many praises to God. Two young men with curly locks led me over to the center of the base of the steps in front of what was as if a pyramid with steps that led upward to a flat region on top. The base of the steps looked to be greater than 50 feet wide. I walked over to the left side as I faced the steps and there the lower steps curved around an upright ornate post with a sphere on top. All the steps, posts, hand railing and spindles at my end and as far as I could see at the other end were white like marble. There were low walls or stairway railing about three feet high with flat stone and a flat stone cap beyond the steps. The two young men sat me down on the second step facing back from where I came. Two young women came forward. One had a hemispherical shaped brass or golden bowl and the other maiden had a large white towel. They placed my feet on their knees and, one at a time, took off my shoes and washed my feet. They were sitting on each side of me. They dried my feet with the white towel and massaged a lotion onto them. I don't remember having any feeling in my feet as they did this. I remember that I thought this was strange. They placed golden sandals on my feet. Then they placed my feet on the ground which appeared like a white marble patio.

Some of the children did somersaults and played around hoping to catch my attention. I believed they were just being children. When I turned around and I looked upward, I could see two bold ferocious golden lions on the three foot wall. The stairway railing or wall was over 2 feet thick. They were at each side of the stairway meaning there was an exact looking stone wall on the other side of the stairway. The lions roared out several times and then sat down. This slightly frightened me. I heard a growling noise so I turned back around to see two older men leading two large bears towards me. They were on bright red leashes with red collars about their necks. The collars had silver medallions on them. One bear was brown and the other was white like a polar bear. The bears stood up on their back legs in front of me and growled loudly. They were at least 12 feet tall on their hind legs. That was a wonder to behold. I did not fear them though because the bears seemed to be tame and gentle. Next, the bears played with the children. The elders then led the bears away from me and the steps.

Several young adults walked up to me. They had very earnest and serious expressions on their faces. They looked directly at me with some trepidation in their faces. They said, "Our Lord awaits you. You must walk up these steps on your own. May your faith keep you safe!" I felt some nervousness and a knot developed in my stomach. Also, again I could hear the thunder and see flashes of lightning. I walked slowly up the steps between the golden lions one step at a time. I remember thinking there was no hand rail. I could fall if I was not careful. This would be bad. I could see a golden radiance like a great holy light shining outward like the sun from the top of the steps up the pyramid. I thought God was up there. It was a strong feeling I had that my fate was in God's hands.

CHAPTER THIRTEEN

MY VISIT TO THE GREAT WHITE THRONE WITH GOD, PART 6

April, 1973

I wrote the full narrative of this vision years later than 1973 on October 18, 1987 from many loose notes that were recorded soon after the vision in May, 1973.

As I looked back on the journey up the mountain it seemed to take only a few hours to travel what at first appeared to be a great distance. I know it must have taken longer than it seemed. I thought of this trip and how difficult it was to reach this location to visit God. I felt a knot in my stomach because the anticipation of meeting our Lord was of much concern to me. I thought how would he judge me? I climbed the steps slowly with deep reverence for our Lord. As I stood up there just one step just below the plateau, I could see all about the top plateau. I could see the Great White Throne with what I assumed to be God sitting on it. I was afraid to take that last step up to the plateau. The throne was here but on the opposite side of the plateau. I counted that there were 32 steps of white marble up to the plateau. I was about 60 feet or more away from God as I stood there on that step just below the top. It seemed to be disrespectful to God to step at the save level as the throne on which God sat. Therefore I stood there just one step down from the plateau or the surface on which God's throne sit.

God motioned to me with his right arm, "Come and meet your Lord." He was smiling very much. He had a look of tremendous approval in his face so I became less tense. I slowly climbed that last step, walked a few steps forward and stood on the plateau. I could see that the throne looked like a large marble chair with solid white sides and arm rests like solid rectangles with veining like marble. The back also appeared to be like a larger solid rectangle with veining in the marble as well. I could see the top above God's shoulders. The back was high enough to enable God to rest his head against it. It was quite simple but beautiful for it glowed alternately gold, silver and light blue. The glow was subdued like a glow candle.

God looked like a very healthy man and he appeared to me to be about the age of 40 to 45 years old. He had a golden tanned face, neck, forearms and hands. As he sat there I could see that he displayed great strength of character and body. He looked like perfection and he had a face with what appeared to be of great wisdom, understanding and maturity. He had on a white light weight robe that draped from his out stretched forearms with his elbows resting on the chair armrests. His robe had golden lining at the neck and forearms and at the bottom near his feet which did not show. He had golden brown hair with blond streaks in it. His hair was very wavy all about and it stood up high and went to the back as if as if the wind had blown into his face. He had exceptionally bronze skin looking very strong in appearance. He was heavily muscled but not to any extreme. Immediately he shone with a golden white light so bright I could not bear to look upon him for long.

Behind the throne were six seraphim angels, each one with six wings. Each seraph angel was about 10 feet tall and had one pair of wings bent downward and forward to cover their feet. Another pair of wings was outstretching to above their shoulders as if for flight and the upper pair was bent upward and forward to cover their eyes. It was as if I could see their eyes but they were also covered. These wings looked like they flickered. The base of all six wings appeared to come from the shoulder blade area of their backs. Each of them had hair that was long and golden draping downward nearly to each of their waists. They wore white and golden robes. The robes were white in background but with much ornamental golden pattern all about especially at their chests which also covered a brilliant scarlet red chest plate. A great white light shone all about them behind and above the throne. That light was very holy and the seraphim sang beautiful songs of praise for God. They sang out, "Praise to God in the highest, for he is most holy. Our Lord's love outshines all. He is love. God's mercy is all knowing. His judgment is good. He will bring you strength. Praise our Lord!" Then God said in a voice that seemed to penetrate my entire being, "Come forward, my son. We will bless you through eternity." At that moment I could see another great white throne at God's right. It was the same appearance as his but was empty. Just below it stood a small pure snow-white lamb. God said, "Behold, the lamb of God!" Above the throne were numerous white doves flying upward and outward to earth. God said, "Behold, the Holy Spirit!" I wish the seraphim angels had told me their names. It would be wonderful to know more names of the important angels in heaven. It does seem odd to me that more persons and angels in heaven do not share their names like the archangels do.

About 10 feet away from our Lord's feet was a great green tortoise that was very majestic standing on all four legs. It was about 2 feet high and was 6 feet long. The tortoise stood upon stout legs. On his back he carried an ornate dark red wooden chest that was two feet wide by one and one half feet deep by one foot high. The corners and edges had ornate gold protective covering on them. The top was dome shaped with gold ornamental art work like the pirates chest. It looked like the typical treasure chest but much more beautiful.

Author's Note: This treasure, I believe, represented the treasure that our Lord Jesus spoke of regarding heaven. Heaven is like a treasure that you strive to

*find in a field. Reference King James Matthew 13:44
(⁴⁴Again, the kingdom of heaven is like unto treasure
hid in a field; that which when a man hath found, he
hideth, and for joy thereof goeth and selleth all that
he hath, and buyeth that field.)*

God peered at me and said, "What will your reward be? We will look into the chest for your reward." He raised his right hand and arm above his shoulders and said, "Behold, your treasure, your reward! Is your heart as pure as gold? Does your soul sparkle like these gemstones? Will you receive your reward here in the Holy of Holies, the living water of refreshment, and the paradise of eternity?" As he spoke, the lid of the chest opened upward over the hinges at the back. I walked further forward to see into the chest. I could see a golden white glow that emanated from inside and there was much gold and many gemstones of all colors within.

Also, at our Lord's feet were two babies playing with toys. They were content and happy and seemed not to notice me. They had very small wings attached on their back at their shoulders. God said, "Behold, the babies in paradise! Have you kept the babies safely and loved them? We will find out. They need your tender mercies."

Then I saw the protectors of the thrones. They were cherubim or two cherubs.

> *Author's Note: These are not to be confused with the
> baby angels which many call cherubs. God refers
> to these baby angels as babies in paradise. These
> cherubim angels are the strongest angels in heaven
> and they once guarded the garden of paradise of
> Adam and Eve.*

The protectors were standing on all four feet on each side of the Great White Throne. They stood in the same stance facing me as if to challenge me. They stood on all fours and each had the face of an angel and the body of a cat like a lioness which is a female lion. I would say their heads and faces were larger than the average person. They each had a pair of wings from their shoulders that were white and charcoal grey and each wing pointed upward about fifteen feet from their shoulders. Their shoulders were about three and one half feet high from the floor. On the wings were numerous eyes with which to see all about and protect the throne. From their forward shoulders emanated arms with hands larger than any human. They gestured very much with their arms and hands as they spoke. To each side of each cherub were twenty feet high wheels of energy with numerous spokes and these revolved forward rapidly. This was an awe inspiring sight to behold.

The cherub at my right and to God's left ran forward quickly to face me. The other cherub followed. Both did not turn when rapidly walking forward but seemed to slide diagonally always with their bodies squarely forward. He said, "We are the protectors of the throne! On your face before your Lord!" I knelt down on my knees and spread my arms outward toward God with my head downward. "Our power is much greater than any other in heaven! A thousand angels could not defeat each of us!" When the cherubim walked it was as if thunder sounded out sharply and the floor on which I stood felt like an earthquake with each step they took it would shake me. When they spoke, it was like resounding thunder that made my bones vibrate. They said, "Now raise your head to us." The one cherub closest to me did turn his head though to face me. Suddenly a dragon appeared far below approaching the throne. The cherub asked me to stand up and he said, "Look below to your right!" Suddenly a bolt of energy shot out from the rotating wheel and destroyed the dragon in the distance with one blast. It was like a laser blast. The bolt of energy was three colors of blue, gold and silver. I was awe struck! The cherub that had displayed the power in his hands said, "That you may know the power of God, you are permitted to see this event! Now kneel before your Lord God and wait your judgment!" I backed up and knelt on the plateau as the cherub said and waited but a few moments.

Author's note: I have noted that many persons do not know what a cherubim is or what they look like. These cherubim are certainly direct and no nonsense angels. They are like angels with enormous energy ready to fight should God be in danger. I was most impressed with them. Ezekiel describes them in the Bible but what he saw was a little different. He saw them with four different faces. That was a symbolic representation for his benefit at that time to convey a message for his prophesies. I saw them as they really are with the faces of an angel. I have included a sketch of one of them within this book so that all will know what they are and what they look like. I regret that they did not tell me their names.

God then spoke up, "Who will speak for this person? What are his deeds? How has he done?" I waited to see what would happen. Suddenly, an elder stepped in front of God and said in a frank manner, "I will speak for him." He looked like the elder who had led me on the path to this throne. I did not know his name or who he was. The elder spoke on, "He is a good person who has many good deeds to speak of, but he did not defend our Lord Jesus to the world so Jesus does not speak for him." Then the elder explained my life in a summary to God. This elder and some of the others I have seen I presume are the seven which the Archangel Gabriel told me would follow me and protect me when I was saved.

After what seemed like hours God said, "It is done, I will judge him! You will have your place in heaven as a *soldier in the Temple of God.* Step forward and kneel." As I did a very majestic angel in a golden armor suit and long wavy golden hair that stuck out in all directions but forward appeared after a loud thunder clap and a blinding flash of light. He had majestic wings that rose to height of about 7 feet above his shoulders. His wings were much more broad and longer all over behind him. This was much different from the other angels I had seen for his wings displayed great golden force and power. His height to the top of his head exceeded 7 feet, and I could see he was very strong. His face shone with golden auras and he had blue eyes, thin lips, a small nose and a holy look in his face.

He said, "I will christen thee before our Lord so that your strength may be increased by our Lord." As he said this he drew out from a sheath a five foot long silver sword that gleamed of light and glowed like the sun. He placed it alternately on each of my shoulders. God said, "Michael, he is in your charge. You must protect him." The Archangel Michael replied, "He will carry the lamp of compassion and care for those who suffer. He has mercy for the weak." At that moment God said "It is done; give him the lamp of compassion and mercy." At that moment I could see and hear the seraphim behind the throne light up the heavens and a large host of angels sang praise to God and his great wisdom.

The next thing I realized I was back on the couch in my living room. There was a great feeling of euphoria within me. I felt in me a message that God is love. In my salvation there flowed from me a great many poems to express my new soul and place in the world. I can only say to you that I was inspired so much by this event that I felt there were angels standing behind me helping me to write down these events and the poems which are included within this book. I had seen God and he has great love and endless compassion. He filled me with love and compassion so much that I could only release these feelings into poems where I celebrated with happiness and exaltation.

Note: Energy wheels are expaneded to show view of cherub. Two cherub are cherubim.

The Cherubim at the Throne of God

CHAPTER FOURTEEN

THE MYSTERIES OF THE UNIVERSE ARE REVEALED TO ME, PART 7

April, 1973

This vision continued. I wrote a full narrative of this vision years later on October 18, 1987 from many loose notes that were recorded soon after the vision in May, 1973.

After I visited the Great White Throne of God, I again found myself on my couch. I thought the vision from God was finished, but it was not. Next, two angels came to me again. After all, what could be more of a climax to the vision than actually seeing and speaking with God himself? The two angels each carried my spirit body which I noticed had the same feelings and thoughts as my earthly body. They had their hands and arms about my upper arms and they carried me up and above the city of Dayton, Ohio in the evening night air. I remember the sensation and exhilaration as if I was riding a roller coaster as they carried me upward quickly. I could see the lights of Huber Heights, Ohio all about.

At the higher altitudes I could see all the lights of Dayton. The dark sky and twinkling city lights blended into one as the main light that I begin to see was the stars. The angels pointed into the upper atmosphere of the earth and said to me, "Look at your future event. This will show you time is controlled by God and he can have whoever he wishes view the past, present and future." I saw the United States shuttle take off and then terror filled my eyes as I watched as the solid fuel rocket boosters separated from the shuttle. Everything spun about in all directions until it all fell back into the ocean. Years later I actually saw via television cameras the breaking apart of the shuttle. I felt sad for the astronauts and especially the school teacher selected to visit space on this flight and the fate of the space program. On the other hand, my faith was greatly reinforced because only God could have shown me this future event exactly as it finally did occur. Now I knew my messages from God and heaven were real and true. My faith in God and his visions to me were real.

Author's Note: The Space Shuttle Challenger disaster occurred on January 28, 1986, when the Space Shuttle Challenger broke apart 73 seconds into its flight, leading to the deaths of its seven crew members. Christa McAuliffe was the first member of the Teacher in Space Project and the first female teacher planned to go in space. The spacecraft disintegrated over the Atlantic Ocean, off the coast of central Florida at 11:38 EST. I saw this in a vision in the spring of 1973. I had told many persons in the mid 1980's that one of the shuttles was going to come apart, but I did not know which one. After this happened then my friends at work believed I really saw this future event.

Then with astounding speed we raced further into the universe and the lighted disc of the earth's moon grew rapidly larger. The angels then set me down in a basin in the middle of a large moon crater that faced the blue earth. I stood there wondering why I was not freezing or dying from the lack of air to breathe. The landscape was an eerie gray and there was a wall of mountains in the distance that were reddish black looking like drapery. An elder dressed in a rough beige robe with a long white beard approached me. He had no hair on the top of his head. He had a serious look of great concern in his face. He stood close by me and asked me, "Is this the place you seek? Do you see the lamp of life here? You see there is nothing here for you or for mankind. This soil will not bring forth life. The sky will not bring forth the refreshing water. This land is dead. But God could give life if it pleased him. Let me show you how life started in your world."

Adam and Eve Forsake God

The elder said, "He brought life to your earth. That pleased him. He brought mankind the garden of paradise. Look and you shall see what I mean." Immediately I could see the garden of paradise that was surrounded by many angels and a fence of clouds. At the entrance stood the cherubim *(Note that cherubim is plural for cherub.)* with high wings and wheels of energy at their sides. They had the face of angels. Below their wings they had bodies like the lioness which is a female lion and they had arms with human hands. Each carried a shield in their left hand and a lance in their right hand. Then I saw Adam and Eve in this garden of paradise. The serpent took Eve's attention and soon they both ate the forbidden fruit. The serpent let forth a hideous laughter of satisfaction. An earthquake shook the ground. All the angels departed and God's anger rained down on the garden. Suddenly, the garden was no more and was replaced by an arid desert. The happy look in Adam and Eve's faces was replaced by pain and despair. Adam and Eve had to live in a cave for protection and eat the plants and animals that were scarce. Adam and Eve had children.

Then I could see men and women multiply upon the earth, but they were all in despair as well. Life was very hard since water and food were scarce. No one knew fulfillment. Then God in his infinite mercy let loose a river of life down the middle of this desert. All who drank of the river of life from God found a purpose in living. The compassion and mercy of God slowly came back over the earth, but he would not give back everlasting life to any person. Then the Son,

Jesus who was sent by the Father took all the sins of men and women upon his breast. Jesus died on the cross and dissolved all the sins of men and women so that we may have everlasting life. When it was done, the spirit of God rained down on the earth again that whoever may choose to drink of the river of life may find everlasting life and fulfillment from God. But everlasting life would only come to those who lost their earthly bodies if they believe in God and were saved. The vision of the evolution of men ended. This was a vision within a vision.

The Mysteries of the Universe Continued

The elder said to me, "No, you will not abide here on this barren world called earth's moon. This is not for you." The two angels took me under my arms again and lifted me up. I was carried over the mountains and we went around to the dark side of the moon. From high up I could see many very rugged mountain peaks all about. The angels said, "Let us leave this darkness for the light." We traveled at a great speed to another world. We were above the surface of Jupiter. I could see the moving orange and red atmospheric belts that were all around this huge planet. I could also see numerous lightning bolts striking in the atmosphere all about. A moon moved nearby us so that we were between it and the planet Jupiter. Suddenly a huge lightning bolt of tremendous proportions struck the planet Jupiter appearing to come from this moon. The angels said, "See the power of God who can create this majestic world." Then we moved quickly to Saturn and the angels carried me right through one of the rings nearest the planet. I could see countless thousands of rocks that were silver, grey, white and black all about the ring. Most were 2 or 3 feet across and were very irregular in shape. The angels said, "Our Lord created this halo to honor Mary, the mother of God, who received this glory from God."

It only took another few minutes and we went closely by the planet Uranus. It was bluish green like a jewel and had a dark belt of coal-like rocks circled the planet several times. Astronomers would call these rings. The angels said, "See, the glory of God that is endless."

Authors Note: Years later a satellite probe went by this planet showing these rings and they were just discovered at that time. By 1978, nine distinct rings were identified. Two additional rings were discovered in 1986 in images taken by the Voyager 2 spacecraft, and two outer rings were found in 2003–2005 in Hubble Space Telescope photos.

All of this was discovered after my vision in the spring of 1973, so again my faith grew stronger.

We then were quickly lifted to a small world named Pluto. The angels set me down on this world on the edge of a lake of ice and snow. The ice lake was very huge. The lake went into the distance as far as the eye could see. I could see an entire dark maroon colored mountain range in the distance very far away. On the side of the frozen lake which I stood, not too far away from me; there was a large mound of rocks that resembled quartz crystals of immense size. These were embedded into the dark rock-like substance. I looked at the sun and it dimly twinkled in the distance. It appeared as only another large star now.

Author's Note: There is now a satellite probe heading for this dwarf planet to show in more detail what it looks like. In 2006, NASA sent a spacecraft to the solar system frontier. The New Horizons spacecraft is now halfway between Earth and Pluto, on approach for a dramatic flight past the icy planet and its moons in July 2015. I hope my faith is again verified as Pluto looks to the probe how it looked to me.

This elder who resembled the one from the moon approached me again. He may have been the same elder. The elder spoke to me, "You now stand at the edge of your system of worlds. Do you see how the light here is very dim? No, you should not abide here either. God loves you too much to abandon you here where you would really be alone. You see you are not really alone in your home world. Your world is filled with many others seeking meaning in their lives. Satan only fools you into believing you are alone so fear will overcome you and you will submit to evil. Are your eyes opened? Do you see more clearly now?" This was an incredible place to be, Pluto. Here there were entire mountain ranges of what looked to be precious stones, but they would be worthless to me here. Only their beauty was noteworthy.

Now the two angels came once again and took me by my upper arms. They lifted me upward into the vastness of space at astonishing speeds. We went by other stars of many colors and also a cluster of stars. The angels said to me, "Get ready for an incredible sight." Immediately the angels lifted me up over the top of our galaxy, the Milky Way. I did not know it was possible to travel this fast. This had to be thousands of times faster than the speed of light. I could see a great nucleus of energy that was very orange and red from which radiated spiral shaped arms outward. Even though in space no sound is transmitted, the angel let me hear the energy of the Milky Way galaxy. It sounded like the chugging of a thousand steam freight trains. Intense tubes of energy that were red and orange and yellow streamed outward only to be captured and returned to the nucleus. Most astounding of all, were the immense light blue beams of lighted energy that shot straight outward into space both directions from the galaxy nucleus perpendicular to the geometric plane of the Milky Way. The beams spread so slightly like cones reaching far out into space. The angels said to me, "Are you not glad for the power of God that holds this immense wheel in shape." I exclaimed that I was amazed at the power of God. It is beyond all reason.

Then the angels carried me quickly past many other galaxies of all types and shapes until we were at the edge of the universe. I could tell this because I could not see any more galaxies in the direction we were going. I did not say anything to the angels but I had wished they would give me some time to look and study these galaxies. We came upon this veil or curtain of very light blue that shimmered to and fro like a delicate curtain in the evening breeze and we stopped again. The angels told me that this was the edge of the universe. They asked me to put my head through this veil. I did so and there was nothing to see on the other side, only darkness. They said, "Do you understand that the power of God is with the light. The light is the way. Without the light you are not with God."

The angels then said, "We will now reveal other things to you. Look upward." As I did a great blue spinning orb did appear. I looked upward to it and within it were the images of many persons.

CHAPTER FIFTEEN

THE MYSTERIES OF THE CIVILIZATION OF MANKIND ARE REVEALED TO ME, PART 8

April, 1973

The vision continued. I wrote the full narrative of this vision years later on October 18, 1987 from many loose notes that were recorded soon after the vision in May, 1973. As I pieced together the chronology of the vision God opened up my mind and I recalled more of this fantastic vision. That enabled me to fill in the gaps missing from the loose notes. As I peered into the large spinning blue orb I could see the beginning of mankind. I saw the Garden of Eden first.

The Garden of Eden

The Garden of Eden was filled with great Godly love. I saw the history of the world pass before my eyes from the very beginning of mankind. In the Garden of Eden the mighty cherubim angels sounded the trumpets when sin began. Eve cried out, realized her nudity, covered herself, and ran away as the garden of great peace and beauty slowly turned to rock and desolation. I saw that she had long wavy golden brown hair and blue eyes. But her eyes were now filled with tears. Adam shirked with grief as he realized the great burden of sin he now had placed on himself from his and Eve's transgression. God then showed him the pain and suffering his descendants would have to bear because of his sin. Before there was eternal life and pleasure; now there will be a life of pain and worry. Worries about when food would be available to eat and where would they find shelter. God's love and tender care were replaced by Satan's evil torment. Evil was now unleashed to the world. From that time on men and women would be confronted with good and evil choices that must be made. Man and women would have to decide whether to accept good or sin. Unfortunately men and women loved the evil choices that gave short term pleasure but long term torment so they sinned greatly. There were many terrible acts of sin. War was unleashed upon the world and men and women perished in terrible acts of murder and sin. People were so irresponsible that they committed horrible acts of murder and genocide. Without God people could not take care of themselves. God was horrified so he had to cleanse the world of these evil people.

Noah and the Ark

Wars and sins were great and then when God could stand no more, he unleashed his anger. Did not anyone realize anymore that the world and the miracle of life were God's creations? If God could find just one decent man, he would save him for future generations. God found Noah and he saved him and his family in an ark from the destruction of the world. God showed Noah the path for salvation and released him from sin and his family's sins. But Noah and his family were godly people so God was pleased with his choice. The plants and animals which God found favor with were also saved for God so desired that we share his glory with the godly plants and creatures. I saw the rain and the devastating floods take all evil men and unwanted creatures. God's plan was to defeat Satan and his demons. He would cleanse the earth. While God did give Satan a tremendous setback, he did not eliminate Satan so sin was still in the world even after Noah.

The two angels lifted me up right next to the large orb that was now surrounded by blue halos. Surprisingly, they carried me right into the orb. The next thing I saw was that I was above the ark. The stormy seas were choppy and there were large ten foot waves. Dark clouds were moving toward the bow of the ark. Noah and his wife ran to the very front on the starboard (right) side of the ark and were afraid. I looked on the wooden ark that had a beam which ran the full length of the boat or the keel which was carved in front and back to look like a coiled rope. Also the beam for the ships roof curved downward in bow and stern and looked like a coiled rope. This was a house-like structure in the middle that had slotted open windows all around below next to the covering that was the roof. It looked like the roof on a house and had spilt shingles to keep out the rain. The entire craft was a reddish brown like it was cedar.

Noah stood at the bow on wooden planks at the boats starboard side. He had long black and gray hair with a long black and gray beard covering the center of his chest. He carried in one hand a tall staff that had a knob on top. He was very tall perhaps at over six feet high. His staff was a least 8 feet high. He thumped the staff on the deck and summoned his family. His wife came to the deck followed by her two sons. Another son stood in the doorway. She walked over and stood next to Noah to his right. The sons who came out stood behind both Noah and his wife. The one son who was still at the door said, "Why have you summoned us father?" Noah said, "We are in for a big storm. Evil is in this storm. We must pray. All of us will pray for our safety"

> *Author's Note: Noah's son's names were not given but I looked this up much later and found their names. Noah had three sons. They were Shem, Ham and Japheth.) Also Noah's sons had their wives (see Genesis 7:7) with them on the ark, but I did not see them.*

Noah's wife had long jet black hair, large dark brown eyes above round cheeks and a heart shaped mouth. She was very beautiful. Her hair was wrapped above in a bun and was braided with a gold cord tied in it. She had a dark olive-like complexion. She was large bosomed and wore a dark green dress and a golden vest that was wrapped around her waist. It did not cover her bosoms. The dress she wore underneath this did cover her bosoms.

> *Author's Note: I did not hear Noah's wife's name mentioned. I looked it up much later and I found that her name is Naamah (Source: The Genesis Rabba midrash lists Naamah, the daughter of Lamech and sister of Tubal-Cain, as the wife of Noah, see Middrash Genesis Rabah 23:4 and it also appears in the Bible in Genesis 4:22). Some other sources give different names.*

She resembled the actress Sophia Loren. Noah had a dark gray robe tied with a golden cord. The sons had a look of fear in their faces. Noah was at peace and his wife was confident that Noah would summon help from God and they would be saved. Noah led his family in a prayer to God. He said, "Lord we have done everything you asked. We built this ark. We believe you can save us now from this evil storm. Please give us a sign." Now I know that back then Noah and his family would not have spoken English but then God must have done this so I would understand them.

Then I could see a shaft of brilliant silver light shine down from heaven onto Noah and his family. Only the one son that was at the doorway did not stand in this light. God said, "Because you had faith you are saved!" The violence of the storm suddenly ended and off in the distance I could see a rainbow. The angels who were holding me sang out. Noah and his family looked up at me and the angels and they were awe struck for what they saw was a silver and white dove. They thought I was a heavenly dove. The one son in the doorway ran to his father's side and shouted, "Look father it is a sign of good fortune." Noah said, "Yes, God has sent us a message. We will send out the dove to look for land as God wishes. We are indeed lucky to behold this heavenly dove." Then Noah's wife said, "God sends us his love. We will be safe." I felt like I was an angel for I could fly and when I did, a large golden halo surrounded me.

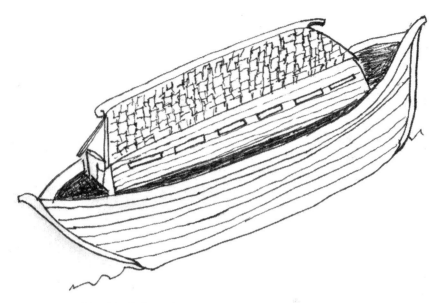

Noah's Ark as it Appeared to Me in a Vision.

Abraham

Next, I was flying above this ancient city. I saw an old but strong and tall man praying to God in a field outside the city. It was shown to me that generations of families had repopulated the earth but all was not good again. The people soon forgot God's wrath in the past and departed from his ways again. God decided to look for another man to whom he would show the path to salvation like he had done with Noah in the past generations. He found a man so good and charitable he was well pleased with him. He found Abraham. Abraham lived among much sin and abuse but he was pure. Abraham believed there was one true God and he believed this God was good. Abraham did not have children, but his faith in God never wavered. He knelt in prayer very often.

So God in his wisdom sent an angel to Abraham and asked him to take his family into the desert away from the golden empire where life was easy but impure. Abraham obeyed the angel and went into the waste lands seeking God. Often he would stop and pray, "God where are you? I love you! You are my rock and my strength! You give me courage!" Abraham shouted this to the heavens. The angel met Abraham again when he was praying at the base of a mountain. A great light shone about the heavenly host. Abraham asked, "What must I do now my Lord?" The angel spoke, "You are the beginning and end. You are the root of life. You will be the life and the way for those who follow. You will begin God's plan. It is good for you are strong in faith. You are the son and the father of God. You are the son of God because he is your father and you are the father of the root of Jesse who is God's son. Behold the Lord of Lords!" The angel showed Abraham his father who is God and his son on the cross. Abraham shouted, "My Lord! My Lord! Why is my son in so much pain? Why does he suffer?" The angel replied "He dies for the sins of all. With his suffering comes the fruit of life; the good in life. It will be good. From Abraham comes a great nation. There will be a nation to collect the words of God for all to know. The way is now clear. It can only be missed by true sinners or followers of Satan."

God did not cleanse the world again but he began a new civilization of people who would be respectful of our Lord and keep the faith. Thus began the Jewish race of Godly persons who found the Lord and kept the records of the encounters with sin and God.

Moses at the Parting of the Great Sea

The vision changed to a later time in history. I could see hundreds of chariots that were chasing after many families who were against a great sea. I saw a man who was Moses standing up on a large boulder praying to God to save everyone from the Egyptian army. I turned to the angel and said, "Can we not help these people." The angel said, "What would you do?" I said, "I would put a wall before the chariots because I do not wish all these men, women and children to perish in this way." I pointed down to the earth and columns of fire dropped onto the earth. Everyone was shocked and the Egyptian soldiers looked up in awe. The fire looked as if it was molten lava. It spread onto the earth and surrounded the families but did not overcome them. The soldiers began to stop their chariots and hold up their hands to shield their eyes from the light and heat of the fires. The people were trapped between the water and the fire. They were all in a great distress and the women and children screamed and cried, "We will die."

The angel said to me, "Now what will be done?" I answered, "Let Moses make a choice by way of his faith." I looked down to Moses and spoke to him saying, "Moses I am here to save you and your flock from the wolves. Your faith will do anything you now ask." When Moses looked upward at me he thought he saw an angel. Moses pointed his rod to the sea and said, "Lord take us to the promised land. We will follow you. I have faith Lord that you will save us!" Then God spoke to Moses so that all could hear, "In you son I am well pleased!" At that moment the water began to move aside and lay a path across the sea for the families to cross. Everyone but Moses was filled with great fear. I saw that Aaron had a very astonished look on his face and then he walked up to Moses and said, "Our God is the one true God of all the heavens and earth! Moses, we must take the people to the other side." Moses beckoned to the large crowd, "See our Lord God is the one true God. We must cross to the other side now." I saw them cross as they went into what had been the sea. A bright rainbow was visible at the other end. This was an awe inspiring sight to behold.

I saw many more events in the history of civilization including David slaying the giant warrior, Goliath. This all went by me so fast much of it was not even discernable. Then the visions slowed and stopped at the mountain where Jesus gave his Sermon on the Mountain.

Jesus at the Sermon on the Mountain

I looked downward and on a hill that was overlooking many thousands of people listening to this man. The two angels held me and the next thing I knew we were about 50 feet above the ground looking at this great event. There was a series of green grassy rolling hills which contained many people. On a hill side stood an immensely important man looking into a crowd of thousands of men, women and children. The man had long black hair draped over his shoulders and that framed a face of great strength. He had a large but not overly large straight nose, dark penetrating eyes and a perfectly rounded jaw with teeth all perfectly in place. He was lean and tall being six feet and one inch in height. I did not measure this but the angels seem to relay this fact to me. As he stood there he was reciting to the multitude of people words of wisdom. On the slope of the hill and at his feet were many children sitting and listening intensely. Below the children were many mothers with their children. Some of the children were crying. There were many hundreds who had traveled all day to see this man and they were standing and were impatient. They were hungry and tired and I could see that they were pressing this man for proof of his authority as a prophet.

Behind this man were about twenty some disciples. They were repeating the words of this man to others so they could hear. Some disciples spoke in other languages to those all around the hill for not all spoke the same language. Two men stood at each side of Jesus as he spoke. I could not hear everything he said but these words that were heard by me are given here. "Peter, he is my rock and the keystone of my good works. He is dedicated to me, and you may place complete trust in him. John he is as my brother and I love him dearly.

> *Author's Note: Jesus does not mean that John is truly his brother, but that he is like his brother.*

When he speaks you may know that truths are revealed. But, John does not have the great strength of faith that is Peters." They were on his right. Then he moved his hands to his left and said, "James my dearly beloved is truth and justice. You may count on James to know the way of the Lord. Follow him!" The fourth disciple said, "Jesus, my Lord, you speak as if you are soon to leave us. You know we love you dearly and do not wish you to leave."

A great warm smile came over the face of Jesus. He spoke to the crowd in a much deeper and louder voice, "See my children, they hunger. We must feed them." The disciples exclaimed, "We have not the food!" The crowd began to get more restless and Jesus turned to a disciple and said, "Philip, how are we going to buy bread so that these people may eat?" Philip answered, "Two hundred denarii's would not buy enough bread for all of them. Then Andrew said to Jesus, "There is a lad here who has five barley loaves and two fish, but what are they among so many?" Andrew ran over to the children and grabbed a basket with but a few fish. Another child ran over to him and picked up another basket with bread in it. Peter shouted, "But how will we feed thousands with only this fish and bread?" These baskets were large being almost four feet where they folded over the food. They were a flat weave, but had rope like edges and large handles that came together from each side. They looked like baskets used to haul firewood.

As I watched on, Jesus stood up very straight and held out his hands and arms as if to embrace all. He said to his disciples, "Make the people sit down." He said a prayer. "Father, so that your children may know you are the Lord, feed them from these baskets. I beseech you to hear my prayer." Then I saw a great white cloud move over Jesus and a brilliant white light shown down all about Jesus and his disciples. There were many shouts of surprise and awe from the crowd. A ten year old child with a disfigured leg limped up the hill and stood within the edge of the white heavenly light. He was struck down and many screamed. Then the boy stood up straight, turned around and walked down the hill being perfectly healed.

Many shouted out, "Look he is healed!" Many shouted Jesus is truly the Messiah.

Many more began to rush forward to be touched by the light. A twelve your old boy rushed up boldly and stood in the light in front of Jesus and shouted, "Do not harm our Lord!" Jesus shouted and it was like the thunder, "Be bold and good like this child!" Jesus then put his hands on the child's shoulders and smiled. Then a voice came from the cloud that said, "In you, my son, I am most pleased." Then Jesus shouted, "Eat, my children, and you will hunger no more. God feeds you that you may know his generosity." Peter and Andrew reached into the two baskets and distributed fish and bread for all to eat. They exclaimed, "Look the baskets are now full!" They walked among the people and the people came forward and took the fish and bread; the baskets became fuller even as they took the food from them. Soon they had to set the baskets on the ground as the fish and bread flowed from them until all had plenty to eat. Everyone ate well that day and all were fulfilled. I could see them sitting on the grassy slopes and they were all satisfied.

When everyone was eating and sitting on the slopes away from Jesus he looked up at me and said with great sincerity, "You see they do not yet understand. I feed them in this way so that they would see how the new word will multiply reaching more people and the word will feed those hungry for the spirit of the Lord. Many will hunger for the word. Eat of my body and you will be fulfilled. And, as more eat, my children will multiply. I tell you this because I want you to tell this to others who will have a greater hunger for my words more than these people. You will tell them.

> *Author's Note: Jesus makes statements similar to this at the last supper before his crucifixion. He means the words of God will feed the hungry souls of mankind.*

Peace be with you, Dennis." I cried because his words were so gentle and soothing to my soul. I said, "My Lord I will remember your words. I will tell them but they may not listen to me." He said, "That is enough. You need only to tell them. They may say they do not listen, but many will."

The angel on my right turned to me and said, "We brought you here so you may know that our Lord Jesus is real and does exist. He did perform this great miracle." I said, "I saw and I believe." Then I looked on as Jesus asked his disciples to gather all that remains of the food into baskets. So when they had gathered the baskets of food, I could see twelve baskets were full. The people looked on and shouted, "This is indeed the prophet who is to come into the world!" They began to shout, "We have found our King, our Messiah!" When they began to press forward, Jesus raised his hands to silence them. They were quiet again and the disciples of Jesus walked into the crowd offering prayers and words of comfort. Jesus left by himself and so he walked into the hills.

This very lengthy vision was then finished. I had seen very much this time. My faith now was even stronger. I have been asked by an angel to spread the Word of God and write down what has happened in as great a detail as I can remember.

I went about for weeks after this telling people that the secret to God is love. Many had puzzled looks in their faces. I prayed very often and felt much love and compassion within me. Also, for many nights after this I could feel the presence of many heavenly angels and persons about me especially when I went to bed in the evenings. The vision was burnt into my soul not to be forgotten, but only more reinforced with time. Every time I would open a Bible, walk into church or pray it would be there comforting me.

I prayed to our Lord. "God now I wonder what you want from me. So while I wait to know your will, I will write down this vision as the angels have asked me. God should you will it, I will release it for the benefit of others. Amen"

Chapter Sixteen

I am Saved and I am Joyous (Poems Inspired by the Angels)

April through May, 1973

God did seem to install into my soul many poems of great exuberance upon being saved. I recorded as many of these as was physically possible. I worked late into the night for several weeks until my spirit was exhausted. I was inspired to write the following poems.

A Prayer to Rejoice for My Salvation is Fulfilled
By Dennis Wayne Schroll, June 1986

Today I feel like rejoicing, my Lord!
Once my sanity was almost lost
Even my wife and family's support left me
My life was in shambles and confusion reigned

But, Lord you came along and took me
I said Lord "I believe! I have faith in Jesus!"
You said "Step forward, my son."
Stepping forward fills me with joy

Lord you took me and said "Believe and you will receive!"
Look at my life now full of blessings
And the Spirit has filled me for all eternity
God bless the Son and my love to the Father

Those hardships showed me deeper meanings in life
Losing loved ones showed me how love fills me
And now, those hardships seem dear to me
My Lord, let me tell others of your gift

My prayers are for our brothers and sisters
They are for those in need of your mercy
My Heavenly Father show those in need
Let me take your loving grace and heal them
                    In Christ's name, Amen

Only a Sunset
By Dennis W. Schroll, May 3, 1973

The sunset was aglow with gold
To remind all to know the day is old

Clouds drift apart, but are part
      Blue sky turns grey, then to haze

Pearls, pillows, warmth, darkness
Silver, blue, gold a part of it

And in the son, life is eternal
When all is done, death is eternal

The streaks of light dance away
Goblets of glows glance astray

Fleeting outward and stretching away
Light that turns to darkness this day

The reminder is written on a cloud
A dazzling multi-colored rainbow
The universe has left for those who see to know

That time does not end for those who seek this
It will be found with bliss!

Where Does It End
By Dennis W. Schroll, April 7, 1973

And some said, she was dead
I knew all along, she had gone beyond.
The life she shed, to be led
With thoughts to belong, to be loved and known

For in living she was giving
Love to me that I may be
A part of her to serve her
It was my goal that I might know
Love … Love … Love

And you know she took a part of me
She took a part of my heart
And left behind a shadow on mine
I'll always miss her and love her
And when she died, I cried … cried

On this Valentine's Occasion
By Dennis W. Schroll, May 3, 1973

I took this class to study art
And then you came along and stole my heart
I hope that we will never part
For along with you would go my heart

What I feel for you, is great admiration
And when I see you, I feel aspiration
You can look at me and see how much I'm shaken
But that I love you with all my heart cannot be mistaken

To Marianne I Give my Heart
By Dennis W. Schroll, May 3, 1973

And when some met
      They shared idle gossip
      They shared affection
      They shared their weaknesses
      And some shared love
      What did we share?

And when some liked each other
      They shared their pleasures
      They shared part of their lives
      They shared each other in their thoughts
      And some shared love
      What did we share?

And when some fell in love with each other
      They shared their secrets and dreams
      They shared their friends and loved ones
      They shared their life and their soul
      And some shared love
      What did we share?

Love I hope.

A Christmas Thought
By Dennis W. Schroll, May 3, 1973

What if ...
        A church was no longer a church
                Farmers kept in them, their hay storage
        Bales stacked high to great beams of birch
                Through the windows
                Could be seen endless varieties of forage

        Happy screaming children were all around playing
                Unknowing they were not Christians
        In those pews they would not be staying
                Their parents were told
                But they knew better and would not listen

        The world is falling apart with decay
                Living is not organized but free
        People loving one another who cannot say
                My country 'tis of thee
                Sweet land of liberty

        In the cornfield is a large scare crow
                Draped over a great ... cross?
        Jesus, only he can know
                That everything has been gained
                And nothing is lost
                Merry Christmas to all

If God Could See Our Love
By Dennis W. Schroll, May 3, 1973

I do not ask that you promise
Your heart in fulfillment of our love

I do not want you to promise anything
Just be honest with yourself,
       And follow your heart
Then if you say to me that you like me,
       It would make my ears ring
I would then know that of me you are part

If our love could shine three thousand miles
Surely it must touch all those in between
To make their day happy with lots of smiles
If it were to shine bright and transcend the heavens,
       What would that mean?

If I could hold you in my mind
       And touch you with time
And if God could see our love
       Then I would know we were seen above
To hold the glow of love in heaven
       Looking back together we ascend

The Message in a Waterfall
By Dennis W. Schroll, May 3, 1973

I love to hear the music of a waterfall
The sun is shining and the wind is blowing
And above the water the trees rise tall
Look at all that water
      Where is it going?

Moving slow and heavy like bass drums
Suddenly everything is alive
Sheets of water intertwining into flumes
And look at all those different drops
      And their size

The release of energy is much like a feeling
It grabs onto your mood and sets it at ease
And the pool below, what is it willing?
That all should be in harmony
      And peace

The Silver Bird Flies, version 1
By Dennis W. Schroll, May 3, 1973

Suddenly, there in the space there was nothing
A new awareness was formed, and it was free
A large silver bird with long sweeping wings,
New things to experience all around and to see

Flying high and wide many wonderful things revealed
And matching one encounter with another, it was fun
That all life must return to the life cycle
But returning is not easy and is met with rebound

Oh, what is it that I am
For what purpose is it that I am here
I would be glad to return if I only knew where to land
To whom do I belong and who can I be near
I really would land if only I knew where

And once again the silver bird spreads its wings
Long silver feathers vibrating to motion
All set into harmonic flutter until they begin to sing
Where to go now? I have no notion

Oh, what is it that I am
For what purpose is it that I am here
I would be glad to return if I only know where to land
To whom do I belong and who can I be near
Flying I hold to be dear, but living I await in fear

Here it is, rolling and floating I am in touch
Wave forms moving and glancing about
I'm in a flux of energy which is almost too much
But I have lost my freedom that I cannot do without

So up to a new level I transcend
Increased in knowledge I fly in heavy air
Here everything is smooth and mellow and oh the wind,
    the wind
Flittering here and about, I'm sad but happy that I'm there

Oh, what is it that I am
For what purpose is it that I am here
I would be glad to return if only I knew where to land
To whom do I belong and who can I be near
I know it now, I am there and I am here

In reaching a new high to the spectrum of purple
Nothing can know the enlightening encounter
But why must I fly alone and why was I chosen
I want to be with life to be near

Oh, what is it that I am
For what purpose is it that I am here
I would be glad to return if only I knew where to land
To whom do I belong and who can I be near
One day I will find out and all will be clear

Posing with outstretched wings in anticipation of landing
Transcending purple, yellow, blue, white down … down …
    down
Over hills of white snow moving swiftly but meandering
There it is! I know what I want, it is found

Swiftly breezing in, ready at last to know
Life is met head on with great expectations
Upon landing it could not be known that it was only snow
The vision was great but it was only a revelation of sorts

A revealing panorama of mountains, high and low
A cresting hill of green trees covered with snow
I can make it, I can make it
The pulse, the throb, heaving about in an easy flow

Trip Out (The Silver Bird Flies, version 2)
By Dennis W. Schroll, May 3, 1973

Suddenly, in the space that was nothing
A new awareness was formed to be free
The silver bird with great swept wings
All around, new things to experience and see

Flying high and wide many wonderful things revealed
Relating one encounter with another, it was found
All life must return to the life cycle
Returning is not easy and is met with rebound

Oh what is it that I am
For what purpose am I here
To just return, but where to land
To whom do I belong, to be near
I would land if only I knew where

Once again the white bird parts its wings
Long silver feathers vibrating to motion
Set into harmonic flutter rising to sing
What is the direction, I have no notion

In reaching a new high to the spectrum of purple
None can comprehend the enlightening encounter
Rising and falling shades of gleaming rainbows
And to ride a comet, unsurpassed is the thrill

Oh what is it that I am
For what purpose am I here
To just return, but where to land
To whom do I belong, to be near
Once this is found all will be clear

Posing with outstretched wings in anticipation of landing
Transcending purple, yellow, blue, white down ... down ...
    down
Over hills of white snow moving swiftly but meandering
The location ... to land here ... It is found

Swiftly breezing in, ready at last to know
A revealing panorama of mountains, high and low
A hill crested with pine trees coated with snow
To make it ... to touch earth
The pulse and throb heaving about in an easy flow

Oh what is it that I am
For what purpose am I here
To just return, but where to land
To whom do I belong, to be near
Flying is dear, but living I await in fear

Here it is ... rolling and floating I am in touch
Glowing wave forms moving and glancing about
The vibration flux of energy is almost too much
Looking at the body with it speeding is without

Soaring to a new level I transcend
Increased in knowledge, moving in heavy air
Where all is smooth, mellow ... Oh, the wind, the wind
Flittering to and fro ... here now and later there

Oh, what is it that I am
To just return, but to land
To skip on a dune of sand
Would someone reach out with a hand?

Johnny Neau

By Dennis W. Schroll, May 1973

This is the plight of one
Who has set aside his gun
    The fight was over
But living had just begun
    Living was a new war
    And live he would

Yes, Johnny Neau was a new man
He had encountered the worst and all he outran
    In fighting he savored
Death and destruction bringing life down like quicksand
    A new world he favored
    And find it he would

All life is precious and dear
It's all about loving and being near
Now Johnny had cast away his fear
He fashioned the word love for all to hear

He now danced to a new song
The rhythm was set to all and one
The tune was in how to belong
Oh yes, Johnny how can you go wrong

Others will sing of Johnny Neau
The tune to be known by a chosen few
Songs to be sung, both old and new
Now this is the plight of Johnny Neau

Goals in Life, version 1
By Dennis W. Schroll, May 3, 1973

When life is spinning to a standstill
And all you have to share is your memories
The time has come to find new dreams to fulfill
And strive to make a pleasant reality of the stories

For living on memories is to cease living
And the telling of stories is not in giving
Just remember to bring cheer
     In the moments of others
They will hold these moments dear
     Thinking of us as brothers

Write in your book new pages
     Each day a new paragraph
     And each year a new chapter
All chapters of the book are by what our Lord judges

And when you reach for fulfillment in life
     Being happy for others
Remember only to push aside the strife
     To love all your brothers

The Journey to Never
By Dennis W. Schroll, May 3, 1973

Trips are taken
    With burdens that must be carried
When life is forsaken
    The encounter can now be varied

For in dying
Can be seen flying
To release the mind
From the burden of time

And without to speed past
Released, with freedom at last

To feel sight
And touch light
In the journey to forever
The endeavor is to be never

Fleeting and swiftly moving past
Unbounded, with freedom at last

Where dreams are told
With thoughts to be sold
    And once being young
    I am now old
    The short life is undone
    To travel on a new road

Soaring high and streaking past
Unchained, with freedom at last

For my mind
Cannot see time
With my body cradled
It will thence be fabled

That in his journey to forever
What he reached was the life of never

The Burden Unloaded
By Dennis W. Schroll

In dying I can see flying
To release my mind from the burden of time
To speed past with freedom at last

I can feel sight and touch light
And in my endeavor to journey to forever
I will fly past with freedom at last

Dreams are told and thoughts are sold
And once being young I am now old
These thoughts are headstrong, I can be bold

For my mind cannot see time
With my body cradled
It will thence be fabled
That in his journey to forever
When this will be reached is never

And Heaven and Earth Agreed
By Dennis W. Schroll, May 21, 1973

The suit of armor gleamed
    In the dazzling sun
He stood with great dignity it seemed
    When the battle was done

Tall he stood with tassels streaming behind
    A saber clutched in his hand
Betrothed and praises he would find
    In this noble promised land

Kneeling to the king he received glory
    On his shoulder rested a star
In a lake of swans glided a dory
    A golden hair maiden from afar

From her face enchanting beauty shone
    Casting the spell over all
The great knight looked and saw the tone
    In no way would they part, by no law

When he touched her hand the earth quaked
    So all knew the feeling
And when he touched his lips to hers the heavens waked
    The impact of loving was chilling

All who looked on saw the wonder
    Praise them, may they never part
When they united the heavens rolled with thunder
    Radiations of love, a new life to start

And with this hand, a part of your heart
  I take thee to be my wife
To love and cherish, may we never part
  Through eternity as one, this is our life

Inward and outward, they imparted a glow
  To others the feeling was good
The vow is sealed with a kiss for all to know
  Two and one was how they stood

From thence on it would be told
  That heaven and earth agreed
The glow of love was beautiful to behold
  From thence on to be together is their need

Miscellaneous Thoughts (Goals in Life, version 2)
By Dennis W. Schroll, May 21, 1973

When his life had spun to a standstill
And all he had to share was his memories
It is time to find new dreams to fulfill
To make a pleasant reality of the stories

For living on memories is to cease living
And the telling of stories is not in giving
Only remember to bring cheer in the moments of others
And they will hold these moments dear and think of us as
    brothers

Write in your book new pages
Each day a new paragraph
And each year a new chapter
All chapters of our book is by what our Lord gauges

Remember but do not forget
Love and move on
Live but do not beget

He had many loves to bring down his pride
How all seems forsaken not worth fighting

And when you reach for fulfillment in life
        Being happy for others
Remember only to push aside the strife
        To love all as your brothers

The Decision or What is Freedom
By Dennis W. Schroll, May 21, 1973

There was one who had a yearning
To travel far and wide to feel free
But eventually his desires are turning
To find a home where others would let him be

In the winds of change there must be a decision
For footsteps can only travel one road
And to take neither would be the same as prison
If only … If only he could be bold

Reason had it that both ways were good
A home could be shared, and traveling was alone
If he could have both lives, If only he could
The adventures of roaming; the peace and quite of a home

Caring for Her Environment
By Dennis W. Schroll, April 7, 1973

Set the scene for a sensuous young girl from the country that is sensitive to her total environment.

Due to lack of funds she is forced to move to the city. She encounters lust, greed, hate and all the various forms of degenerate human emotion.

She begins to feel bitter and lonely.

Many reproach her and she doesn't understand why everyone seems so hard and resentful.

She sees hippies preaching love and peace and takes up with some girls and they in turn become involved with others.

She has found a beginning to belong to a group with common interests and goals.

Life improves and she becomes herself again, sensitive to her total environment.

Then some people judge her to be less than they are. She is different but happy.

Remember now she is the wiser one in this city. Remember that before you judge someone who is different.

The Forest Changes
By Dennis W. Schroll, April 7, 1973

The birds in unison stopped their song
A great black cloud looked menacing in the distance
The rabbits scurried into the brush for cover
The terrible storm was coming, it would not be long
What would happen in the forest that is left to chance?
A threat to life is in the process, but refreshes life when over

Freedom to Breathe,
By Dennis W. Schroll, April 7, 1973

I know a town
Where life is down
And love is only a frown

To climb above this all
   I must try
Show me where is the law?
   I must cry
Bitterness, guilt, and hate I saw
   Just makes me sigh

Oh, my life is too short to waste
With people to bitter to taste
Whose souls seem to be lost in the haste
And appearances look to be but paste

I want to know what happened!
Looking down a road laden with hate
Was I previously told this was my fate?

I just can't remember the lesson
For I would have asked the question

Where are love and the white dove?
Does it only exist in heaven above?

Where is happiness, is it all past
I demand the freedom to breathe, to have it last

I know a town
Where life is down
And love is only a frown

To climb above this all
   I must try
Show me where is the law?
   I must cry
Bitterness, guilt, and hate I saw
   Just makes me sigh

If Loving You
By Dennis W. Schroll, May 21, 1973

If loving you wants you in everything I plan
And wanting to be close to you as often as I can

If loving you is treasuring each moment that we share
Because you bring me happiness that's beautiful and rare

If loving you is missing you whenever we're apart
And needing you is to help fulfill the dreams within my heart

If loving you is trusting you and caring so sincerely
If loving you is all of this I love you very dearly
When I reflect into my heart I see you very clearly

That must be true love
Love from heaven above

You are the one in my heart
We surely can never part

CHAPTER SEVENTEEN

VISION OF LUCIFER TEMPTING ME AWAY FROM GOD AND HIS ANGELS

June, 1973

I wrote this on December 23, 2011. This vision occurred several weeks after the visit to the Great White Throne. This vision had always troubled me so I did not write it down soon after it happened. After all, who wants to remember a visit from the master of evil himself, Lucifer? However, I have decided to include this because it really did happen and it is a big part of the story. I have struggled when making decisions in my life between good and evil choices. Sometimes evil choices do not seem evil or bad because Satan tricks you into believing it is good. The struggle between good and evil is difficult.

This vision is as clear in my mind as if it were yesterday when Lucifer tempted me not to listen to God and his angels. It was summer in 1973. I was living in an apartment in Huber Heights, Ohio. I had heard the news from God when I was at the great white throne. I had heard his words of encouragement and our Lord's happiness when I had turned away from evil. I did this when I was at the gates of hell. I called for God's help.

I was standing in the kitchen. I heard some noise at the front door. The front door was a right turn out of the kitchen into a hallway which goes to the bedrooms and entry door. I turned and went down the hallway and turned right again towards the entry door to the apartment. I looked straight on at the apartment exit and entry door. I stopped quickly.

There in front of me was the most beautiful angel I have ever seen. This angel had very white skin and a face much like that of a china doll with a small upturned nose. The angel had golden hair drawn back in multiple braids on top and back of his head. The angel had his hands together at his lower abdomen and he had a slight smile on his lips. This did not appear to be a smile of happiness but the kind of smile you see when someone is upset with you. His white and gold wings were to his sides and upward about 5 feet above his shoulders. This was the first time I recalled seeing an angel with gold on his wings. He wore a light blue robe which seemed to be illuminated from within and behind. He wore golden sandals and a golden braided rope around his waist. He was illuminated from behind with a very light golden light nearby his person but was also illuminated from behind this with a brighter nearly white light. The light glowed like a three pointed star with one point upward and to the left and right of his shoulders. It had the appearance of starlight.

The angel did not identify himself but began speaking to me, "You should not listen to God and his group of mindless angels. They only have your destruction in mind and they wish to make a mockery and fool of you. Listen to me and I can provide you with anything you wish. I can make you rich and powerful. I am an archangel of great power. I have power that is greater than any other archangel and even God himself. We will make a great team fighting God so that he cannot make a fool of you." He was dissatisfied with my decisions recently. I could not believe what I was hearing from an angel. Was he from the Lord I thought? I said, "I do not know what angel you are but you must not be from God so I think I cannot trust you. I have faith in God and his angels. I know he loves me and intends only wonderful things for me." I did not immediately know but this was Satan in his angelic form and he had evil intent with me.

The archangel then replied, "You will be fooled. You will have a life of misery and despair here in this world. God will not save you from this. You will regret listening to God. He only wants you to live in misery, despair and unhappiness." I said, "I know the road to heaven is not necessarily an easy road and I'll have many struggles to overcome. God has assured me that with faith in him I will prevail. His angels have saved me many times from harm and even hell itself." The archangel then said, "You are a fool and I can defeat any fool and win you over." I said, "What do you mean you can defeat me?"

The archangel began to throw a tantrum and slowly changed into a different form. He looked as if he had the body of a man with great muscles and he was dark brown skin all over. He had the head of an angry bull with long round horns to the side that curved upward. He looked like a Minotaur in Greek mythology. He then snorted loudly and grabbed my upper arms and threw me against the hallway walls. He then tired of slamming me about and threw me to the floor. I felt very sore but I arose and said, "You do not scare me!" We then wrestled back and forth on our feet for what seemed like fifteen minutes or a longer time. When I looked upward I could see fires burning in a distance above me. I could see all sorts of ugly demons shouting and wishing my defeat.

I began to see that I could not win this battle alone so I yelled out loudly, "God is my savior and protector. I ask for his help to save me from this terrible thing and the demons all about." I then heard trumpets blazing and from behind me in the living room, the Archangel Michael came forward in a chariot with two horses. The chariot was golden and the harness was also golden. The horses were white and seemed very powerful. Other lesser angels came with the Archangel Michael and they shouted, "Be gone Lucifer. He does not want your empty promises." Lucifer and his demons decided to make a hasty retreat back into some part of the spirit world I know not where. The Archangel Michael then said to me, "You are free of this evil one and his empty promises. His demons cannot bother you anymore. We will protect you as long as your faith in God is strong." I said, "I greatly appreciate you saving me from this terrible spirit. You say this was Satan and his demons. I will keep my faith and my love in God strong, that I promise."

I then realized soon after the vision ended that I had been tempted by the fallen Archangel Lucifer himself who we now call Satan. I felt shaky in the knees thinking I could have been lost if I had not asked God for help. Just as Jesus was tempted by Satan I was also tempted. I think many who are renewed with faith in God will be tempted by Satan. They may not necessarily see Satan, but he or his demons will be there. It is my prayer that they keep their faith strong and not fall into a terrible fate with Satan. This was a short vision, but nevertheless a very important lesson I learned from knowing what I had to deal with. Other persons will also have to deal with the temptations of Satan even after they are saved. Godly persons will often need to deal with Satan and his hosts of demons. These demons were once angels in heaven but now they are rebelling against our Lord God. I have researched this and found that Satan is trying to prevent as many persons as possible from believing in God and from wishing to go to heaven. It seems Satan hates our Lord. He had attempted a long time ago to overthrow God and his kingdom.

CHAPTER EIGHTEEN

THE NEED FOR A NEW TEMPLE OF GOD

May 31, 1987

I wrote about this vision soon after it occurred on June 1, 1987. God sent me a vision concerning his temple. While I was sitting on my couch in the living room eating some snacks I looked up and I saw an angel descend from heaven. The angel looked at me with arms outstretched and hands upward as if begging for my attention. The angel said to me, "Do you know what you must do with the old Temple of God." I said, "No, I do not know." I was worried that I gave the wrong answer for he lifted me upward in my spirit body to a place somewhere in heaven. He lifted me without any help which was different because in the past usually two angels would lift my spirit body upward to heaven.

I was now in a place where a temple sat like that built by Israel in the days before Christ. The angel firmly said, "Take this broom." I took the broom. It was a straw broom with a green wooden handle. The angel sat me down inside the temple at the right side of the altar. As this happened, a great cloud of dust stirred about me. After the dust settled I could see a three inch deep carpet of dust all about the temple floor. This did not look like earthly dust because it sparkled and was interesting to watch. The altar sat on fluted columns over a raised panel wooden box. On the altar was an empty golden bowl. In front of the altar was a wooden hand railing with a swinging gate at the middle where the entrance and center aisle came into the altar. I looked out over the railing and I could see a great empty room like a dead church. It was as if the church had been abandoned for years. There were empty pews and up above was a balcony with pews of similar hardwood and (oak) hand railing and turned spindles were at the edge of the balcony to prevent a person from falling over the edge of the balcony. Above the pews up high in the center of the back of the church over the main entrance was a large round stained glass window about 12 feet in diameter. This verily let light through into the darken temple assembly room. I did not know what this temple represented because the angel did not say, but I could say it was a Christian church.

God spoke to me from above the temple roof in a commanding like voice and said, "Do you see this empty temple. My children no longer care about me. Have they been led astray by Satan or do they love their sins? Are not they interested in love and happiness? Why do they seek to only destroy themselves? Let me show you." Then the angel took me by the right arm and lifted me upward. We came back down again in front of another rectangular shaped building which was two stories high. There were pastel red and blue neon lights above the large picture window to the seating area within. The sign said "Surf and Turf, place of God's Forgotten Children." The angel beckoned me to enter. A bar and many wooden tables were inside where men and women of many races were shooting drugs, gambling, planning robberies and drinking alcohol. Upstairs I could see that men and women sold their bodies for pleasure and money. It was a sad sight to behold. The angel looked at me earnestly and asked, "See what they do. They do not enter God's Temple. They seek only to sin and destroy themselves. What will you do?" I answered, "I am angry." I lifted up the straw broom and began to chase everyone about. I said, "I'm angry with you all. If destruction is what you want then I can bring about the destruction you want so much."

As I began to swing the broom about in a rage to hit the sinning people, I suddenly found myself back into the temple. God thundered out loudly, "Judgment is mine! Do not take anger upon yourself. You seek to destroy sin, but you only destroy yourself. Let your love and compassion destroy the sin that is everywhere." Next God said, "You are the caretaker in this temple. Sweep the dust from it." I did as God said. Suddenly the dust turned into silver dust that glowed and twinkled. I saw it lift upward and it was thrown across into the sky as if in a wind storm. It became like the stars in the night sky. There was a stained glass window in the temple above the balcony which looked to be 12 feet in diameter and it was in twelve sections, one for each apostle. It looked like a rose. Then it fell to the floor in a great crashing noise. The broken glass rose window reassembled itself into a 12 foot diameter wheel and rolled out the front door. The roof and ceiling went upward into the sky into a slow spiral until they disappeared into the distance. Then God thundered out, "I am angry, if mankind does not want this temple then it will be destroyed! Let no man put asunder what God has given in love." Then one by one the temple walls fell outward. They crumbled into dust. A great whirlwind picked up the silver dust all about me. I could not see anything. Then God's voice rang out, "It is done." Immediately the dust was gone. I stood on an altar which was twenty feet square that was atop four fluted columns. The columns had scroll work at their tops. It was all as white marble. I stood there with destruction all about me. The temple walls were crushed into rubble. The altar remained untouched where I stood. Apparently God still wants people to come to his altar and pray even though the church is gone. It became clear to me that God's altar is the means of communication between the people and God. It is not the church, but the place where people give themselves to God. I believed God has some mercy for humankind because his altar was still in place.

As I stood there Jesus appeared in front of me and said, "We will build a new temple. I am the foundation and you are the lamp to show the way to my tender mercies. Go out into the world and show everyone who seeks the way to my temple how to find it." Then a great blinding light came from Jesus' face until I could not look upon him. I kneeled and prayed to God for wisdom and strength to do this will. I saw the angel lift me upward into the sky. Over the horizon I could see a rainbow that was above paradise. It was peaceful and beautiful. The vision ended.

I have thought about this vision for years and I still do not understand what the temple really was that God destroyed. If it was the temple in Jerusalem, this was already destroyed several thousand years ago. I have begun to think this temple is a representation of the churches in the modern day world but then I don't completely understand this vision because not all of these churches are empty. Many of them are filled with Christians so I'm still not sure what God is destroying. Maybe God will reveal this to me sometime later. Another thing I do not understand was why God showed me the vision of destroying the old temple after he showed me the vision of the new temple. Maybe he destroyed the first Temple of God he showed me and next he showed me an even better Temple of God for Jesus' return. Maybe there will be a new and better Temple of God for Jesus' return revealed to future prophets. Only time will tell what was the temple in this vision. God seemed to be emphatic about building this temple as he showed it to me three times!

CHAPTER NINETEEN

GOD SENT A VISION ABOUT HIS NEED FOR A NEW ALTAR

June 12, 1987

I wrote this the same day of the vision on June 12, 1987. The Lord God said to me, "I am pleased that a few have found their way to the altar by the dim light of my disciples, prophets, apostles and saints, but I will cast that light down. It will crash to the floor of my temple, but it will not be forgotten."

Then the Lord's angel showed me the sin in the world. I was very sad because these people were bent on self destruction. They cared not for their own souls. Those great sins shown to me were murder, drinking, gambling, adultery, taking addictive drugs for pleasure, the selling of flesh for money and pleasure that included homosexuality, robbery and those who neglected the well being of their families. God said, "I am not pleased. They have turned away from me. They do not want the freedom and happiness I offer. They only want pleasure or vengeance." God said, "Take this broom and sweep the dust of sin from my temple." I did this. I became angry and chased those sinners that I could see from their evil pursuits. As I did this, God said again, "No, you will not be angry. Anger is mine sayeth the Lord God. I have told you this once before. You must learn to love all others." Then God said "I'm angry but my final judgment will not come soon, but it will surely come. I will take down my temple as it is now. The ceiling that is stopping my light will be cast away and all the brilliance that is heaven will be seen on earth by those who look. I will cast down the walls of the temple so that many will easily find their way to the altar. Before my altar could only be approached through the door of life and down the hallway of truth. Now my altar is open from all directions. You must only look upward to heaven for the light to find your way there." As I swept the dust of sin from the temple a great whirlwind of sparkling dust swept around me. God lifted the temple roof and ceiling upward into heaven with his hand. The wall to the left fell outward and crumbled to dust each wall followed it in succession. Suddenly dust was all about me and I could not see.

Then the Lord Jesus spoke to me, "He said gently, "Dennis, Dennis, I have come for you, what will you do?" I said, "Save me Oh Lord for I am a sinner who is not worthy to clean your feet. Why do you want me?" The Lord said, "Kneel, we love you. Heaven welcomes you with open arms." As I kneeled I opened my eyes. The dust was cast to stars in the sky by one outward sweep of his Lord's hand. He said, "Dennis, I cast the dust of sin from you so that you may be the lamp of compassion and mercy. Light the path to me and my altar so that many will know the great rewards in heaven." As I looked about me I was on a slab of white marble that was 20 feet square. I was in the middle and an angel lifted me upward. I could see that the altar was on four great fluted pillars or columns. The columns had scroll work on their tops. The angel lifted me higher and I could see the rainbow of love up in the distance. Under it and behind it was paradise.

God said, "In my new church the altar will be more accessible for many to come, but the sacrifices will be less than I asked from my promised children of Israel. All should mark this day in 1987 as the end of an old era and the beginning of a new era for humankind. This day will be remembered forever. God has forgiven his children. God is love." The vision ended.

This vision resembled that previous vision where God destroyed the old Temple of God. Our Lord is making it very clear to me that there is a basic problem with the existing temple. It must be destroyed so a newer and better Temple of God will be built on earth and heaven. However, new revelations are given that explain that Christ's judgment will be coming. I think God is speaking metaphorically about destroying the old temple. I mean I think he is referring to the way people worship. God also announced that there is a new age and his involvement in the world will be greater in this new age.

CHAPTER TWENTY

THE NEW TEMPLE OF GOD

This vision occurred in the late summer of 1973

I wrote this June 1, 1988 from notes I had made in 1973 soon after the vision. To my surprise as I walked from my bedroom to the kitchen in my apartment in the hallway there were two angels before me. They looked at me with serious concern. Both were as men in their middle age, but they were angels with wings spread above. They each took me by my upper arms and said, "Your time has come!" I felt some fear of the unknown, but my trust in Jesus was my thought at that moment.

They lifted me upward very quickly to a place in heaven. It was no longer my material body but it was my spirit body. There was a brilliant golden light in my eyes so that I could hardly see. I was asked to sit down on a three legged stool of gold with a marble round white seat. The legs were as eagle legs with claws at the floor and they had about them great pearls as great as three inches in diameter. There were many heavenly persons here and angels behind me. There was a thick golden braided rope hung from pedestal to pedestal behind me and to my left. Many angels stood facing the same direction they placed me to face. I could hear there were many angels behind me as well. They stood behind the rope to my left. The two angels pulled me back some and they pulled off my shirt. The angels to my left turned to face me. Two maidens walked beside me and each took my shoes off and then my trousers so that I wore only my shorts. The maidens placed at my feet a golden bowl partly full of water. They washed my feet in the water. As they did all tension left me.

I could hear many whispers from behind me. Angels and heavenly persons also stood behind me. Elijah, the prophet of olden days stepped forward and announced his identity. He said, "You are *"chosen"*. You are the one who is to come before our dear Lord and tell of his coming. You will speak of many wondrous things. Open up your heart and let the Spirit in." Then I heard several angels exclaim, "But will he be strong enough? We would have chosen someone with greater strength." Elijah shouted, "Quite! Do you question the wisdom of your Lord?" They replied, "No! We accept him without any reservations." They said loudly, "Stand, *'chosen one'*!" I did stand and they quickly pulled off my shorts and placed a short loin cloth about me so that my modesty was not violated. The cloth was white satin with a Greek key pattern at the lower edge in gold.

As I stood I could see a long hallway before me with a white marble floor. The marble tiles were about 3 feet square placed end-to-end. There were alcoves or chapels to my right. The crowd behind me exclaimed in unison, "Step forward and accept your duty." Then I stood up straight and tall and slowly stepped forward. My feet had been made clean to walk on the holy floor. In the alcove I could see the burial tomb of Jesus. A great stone was rolled back and two women were on their knees before a stone table on which had laid the body of Jesus but now he was not there. They cried, "Someone has taken our Lord and we do not know where he is." The women could not see that two angels stood in the tomb one having just rolled back the stone and the other holding, draped in his arms, the cloth that had covered Jesus. Slowly I took more steps forward, and next I could see Jesus talking to a woman in a garden. He announced that a new age has begun. No longer will God seek vengeance on men and women. All who seek God by way of Jesus will find him. To love one another is his greatest commandment. He wants his disciples to tell others he has come and what he has said.

I walked forward to the next alcove. Thousands of crosses were burning and it was terrible to see. The apostle Paul stood before me. He said, "I sent out the good word but not all would listen." He exclaimed. "Some placed themselves before our Lord God." In the next moment Paul was in a dark prison and I saw a henchman take his head off with an axe. I walked forward and I could see in the next alcove the apostle Peter upside down on a cross. Peter looked at me and said, "You can see our suffering is great, but our Lord promises a much greater reward. Our faith will be rewarded." I stepped forward again to the next alcove and I could see a peaceful scene where the lion and lamb lie down together. Jesus stood dressed as a Shepherd and he held a tall staff. He said to me, "You will make way for the time when the lion and lamb lie together. You will begin a new age. A time of many miracles and great faith will follow. But, also a time of great suffering for the evil ones who will turn on the good Christians and persecution of believers will spread like a wildfire. You must hold the shield for the Christians who keep their faith to keep them with God. You are the *chosen one* to fight the beast and his demons. When you smite them, God will be in your arms." Then Jesus lit a small candle and placed it in the palms of both of my hands. Jesus said, "Take this candle and light others so that your army will increase, and increase it will for God has promised this."

I stepped forward to the next alcove where there were three candles of different heights. I lit each one of them and said a prayer to God, "Give me the strength to smite thy enemies!" Then seven prophets appeared before me and said, "We will follow thee to light the way for all to see their duty. It is good."

Then I stepped before a great round hall with a dome over a great white altar on pillars. But I did not enter yet. Three soldiers stepped forward and said, "This is the Temple of God and you are a soldier to guard it." They handed me armor, a shield, and a great silver sword.

They laid down a white satin towel and I stepped on it. Two maidens placed golden sandals on my feet. They said, "We will guard your way and keep you strong. When you need us we will be there." I knelt down and said, "I accept my duty!" Then I could see beyond the altar, God sat on a white throne and to his right sat Jesus on a throne just like the throne on which God sat. The Holy Spirit in the form of a white dove flew around the altar and landed on my right shoulder. And God said, "It is done! Go into the world as a *'soldier in the Temple of God'.*"

Then I felt a great duty for righteousness and willingness to battle the evil spirits that came to me. The next thing I knew I was in my apartment sitting on the couch. But from that moment on I knew I would never be the same person. Before I was a man, but now I was a warrior of God.

At times I would reflect back onto this vision and think, "How can God think that I am as powerful as his archangels? It is puzzling to me that he chose me, the one who is always ill, to be such a great warrior." I just keep thinking, "God has more wisdom than I and so I will follow his commandment to slay the evil prince. I know this is some time away when I am but a spirit body and no more a material body in this world." I keep thinking, "My position and duties in heaven must be vastly different than here on earth. But I could be wrong. Maybe God has given me this duty while still in this world. Time will tell me what I must do and when."

CHAPTER TWENTY ONE

THE VISION GIVEN TO ME FROM GOD CONCERNING THE COMING OF CHRIST AND HIS FINAL JUDGMENT

Late April, 1987

I wrote this not long after the vision occurred on May 25, 1987. It had been 14 years since my visions with the angels and God.

My heart feels compassion for those who had not seen the way of God and I asked that Jesus be their Savior. I was thinking this as I sat on the living room couch listening to music. A vision was then given to me of the future day when the final judgment would begin. I was standing in heaven and looking down to the world and the sad state of affairs of worldly things. The angel of doom looked to me and said, "Dennis, the time has come." I said to him "I have tried to save many but they would not listen to me. They were so concerned with their worldly goals and events there were not time for God." I said to the angel and three other angels standing by us, "What time has come?" The angel of doom said, "Look to those clouds. The time for our Lord to take his sheep has come. I must sound the trumpet to announce his arrival." My thought is that this is a future event sometime after I have passed on and left the world. I am a spirit body only.

I looked to the sky and I could see our Lord Jesus riding a fiery chariot above a white cloud with flames trailing behind. He had a great look of compassion and love in his face. He wore a cream colored robe with golden lining and trim at the edges. When I looked into his face I could see great love shining outward and a glow of silver so bright in his face that shone with a greater increasing intensity until I could not bear to look upon him. A white dove was perched on his left shoulder. Jesus' hair was black but it seemed to radiate a red glow like burnt embers from a dying fire. The majestic horses that pulled him were **Thunder**, a blue horse on his left and **Lightning**, a white horse on his right. They had long manes and tails that trailed into the heavenly wind. The chariot and harness were gold and scarlet red. The harness straps were red but the chariot yoke and tongues were golden. The wheels were red but the spokes were gold. In the front of the chariot cab was mounted a great red gemstone that looked like a ruby. There was ornamental gold relief decoration all about the ruby like it was mounted on a plaque.

Jesus outstretched his arms and called for his own. Many of those who were going about their daily activities stopped and went out into the street and the open fields and looked up to Christ. They were happy and shouted, "Glory to God in the highest! We are saved!" Others, who were not saved by their own choice, shouted all about and began to persecute and kill those who were called out by Jesus to live in paradise. They were being jealous and they became evil with so much sin. See the great sin that jealousy causes. Blood covered the ground and streets. It was a tragic sight to behold. As soon as the faithful died, Christ raised them up and they were saved. They were made most holy. I said to the angel of doom before he blew his long straight golden trumpet announcing the coming of Christ, "Why must all these other souls die and not know our Lord's mercy and rewards." The angel said, "They would not listen to you even though you showed them everything about our Lord's gentle ways and his great compassion." I said, "I weep for them." The tears fell from my cheeks with much sadness.

Soon clouds covered all the earth and great torrents of rain fell. Pools of water and mud were everywhere. The angel began to raise his trumpet again and I said, "No wait, give them another chance." The angel said, "You may pick those you can find who are righteous, but they are weak of faith and set them aside. They will be spared." As I cried I did this and they were saved, the most righteous I could find. They numbered only seven. They were two elderly gentlemen, two young male adults, one older lady, one younger woman and a young girl child. Jesus lifted them up to the clouds and they were spared. I could see they were happy knowing they had just been spared. They looked aglow with white holy light as they stood on the edge of a cliff. I could see many trees and flowers in their background. It was their paradise.

The angel sounded his trumpet and another angel of doom passed his hand and arm across the earth. As he did he poured agony and death out from a small vase or vial such that it covered the earth under his shadow. There was death and destruction everywhere. It rained a yellow putrid stench like sulfur everywhere. Pools of yellow water and mud and bodies were everywhere.

Then the angel of doom said to the Lord Jesus who looked on, "They would not listen. They enjoyed their sins." The angel drew a great silver sword from its sheath about his waist that gleamed with light. He held it up, pointed it to Jesus and said, "On your request!" Jesus said, "Let it be done as said in those ages past when I was in agony for all their sins that were great and many. Let them answer for their sins." The angel of doom raised his silver sword of gleaming light and wielded it against the earth. It hit the earth as a wall of fire that burned everything before it. I could hear much screaming as thousands died in agony. Their faces were twisted with pain and arrogance. Their hearts were hardened against our Lord. The sword then laid open a great gaping chasm before it while many earthquakes covered the land. I could hear thunder and see lightning all about. The earth groaned before the sword of justice. Many were consumed, but those who remained panicked and screamed for their earthly prince the son of Satan to save them. In a last attempt by Satan to turn the entire world against God, Satan fathered an earthly child to lead all the persons of the world to their side in sin. I cried tears again upon seeing their arrogance because in their pride they caused their own death.

Then a great charging black bull that was at least 20 feet high at the shoulders trampled towards me along the greatest chasm. This was the spiritual image of the prince of evil. The people said, "He has come. We will be saved!" Jesus said to the people remaining on earth, "You saw me, but you did not see. You heard me, but you did not listen. You saw my power, and yet you did not yield. Prince of evil, son of Satan, they are yours for they asked for your grace. Show them your grace." Then the great black bull with red eyes that seemed to penetrate right through you and with fiery breath, stomped his hoofs down on all those who were left. He stomped them to dust and ashes. They were consumed in pain by the prince of evil. Evil had no compassion and no grace. I was sad for I could see the agony and disbelief that was in their faces.

The prince of evil looked to those seven righteous persons I had chosen and began to stomp towards them. He raged out to heaven, "I took those here, now you are mine as well for they are between heaven and earth. See God is not so great. Look only a few are left. I have taken many already. I will have you then heaven is mine." Those seven said "We fear not for Jesus will save us. God is most powerful." I screamed, "No!" at that moment. I drew my silver sword that gleamed with light and shouted to the evil prince, "You will not harm these righteous souls. You will not have them and you will not harm our beloved Lord Jesus!"

My great steeds **Faith** and **Trust** were harnessed to a gold and red chariot that looked much like the one Christ rode in, but it had a great pearl in front instead. To hasten my rescue I drew my silver sword, jumped forward off the chariot and cut the chariot harness away from Faith and Trust. I grabbed the sword in my teeth and jumped upon my steeds. I rode forward with the reins slapping Faith and Trust to the left, then the right until I could overtake the great black bull. I screamed at the top of my lungs "Faith and Trust will save us!" As I rode towards the prince of evil, I again shouted, "Once you, the evil king had my head, now I will have your head. You, the wretched prince of evil will be stopped!"

Now two heavenly cherubim appeared on each side of the seven righteous souls. The cherubim had the faces of angels, tall wings up from each of their shoulders about 15 feet high with eyes all over the wings for looking all about. The cherubim had wheels of energy of red, yellow and green at each side with radiating spokes included that rotated rapidly forward. The wheels of energy were attached to their bodies which are like lioness and were parallel to their bodies. The wheels moved with their bodies because they were a part of the cherubim. I brought down my sword on the prince of evil, who was in the form of a terrible black bull. The cherubim sent beams of energy with all the force and the power that was in heaven. The beams of energy hit my sword and increased its strength many times. The prince of evil was destroyed as the sword came down upon him.

The sword cut the shoulders, head and forelegs from the body of the bull. Each half laid on their sides and spun around slowly in circles as the life blood went out of the body of the bull. Red blood spurted everywhere and covered my white tunic. I then severed the head from the bull and held it up before Christ. As I did, all heaven sang out, "Praise the Lord for he is most powerful! The deed is done! We are saved by Christ! The *Chosen One* has slain the beast! The prince of evil is no more."

Thus the vision ended.

This was a very colorful and emotional vision filled with much violence and death. It shall be branded in my mind such as the tragic event it is. I shall never forget this vision. Apparently, this is what

God plans for me in the future. I do hope all goes well for the good persons and angels in heaven.

Pray that Love Knows Us

By Dennis W. Schroll, April 9, 1986

When I have love in my heart
    Nothing on earth can take us apart.
When you return to me your love
    I know that Grace comes from above
When I give to you mercy, you return the love of God
    I get on my knees to you and God
My prayers are sent for you and also me
    So God cannot forget those who are humble you see
May our years together be great joy?
    And plentiful peace be with you my love
I hold you gently in my arms today and forever
    So I have hope for our future without sin never
Shall it darken our hearts?
    Or keep us apart
    My love for you may it last forever and ever! Amen

I am a Song
By Dennis W. Schroll, June 1, 1988

In the ripples of time
There is a space I call mine
    You call me a baby
    Then a boy is made
    You call me a boy
    Then a young man puts aside his toys

My space, my time is short
It is good, I am happy to report
    The passage of time made me a man
    Then the spirit of God took me in hand
    Before I was a man struggling with suffering and pain
    But God took my space, my time and I'll never be the same

Now who am I?
    Not a tree or a cloud
    Not a bird or thunder loud
    Not even a fish
    Can you make me with a wish?

I am in God and he is in me
    My sight is good and with the Spirit I can see

So even though my time be short
    My life, my spirit is long
Now who am I . . . I am a song
God sees that my rhyme is in time

A Prayer to Keep My Faith Strong
By Dennis W. Schroll, November 11, 1987

God, I remember what you told me
      That my life would be full of blessings
When I look at my life, all I can see
      Is grief and tragedy, why do you keep me guessing?

I see you can make the roses beautiful in season
      But later, pink petals they wilt and drop away
God, I didn't get my flowers today, what is the reason
      My life has withered; I just don't know what to say

Is it true that without suffering there is no true love?
      Then everyone should sing and shout praise
Because with my suffering and my hurt, it must be great love
      Please bring me happiness my Lord, and bring better days

I do keep you at my side, my hope is strong
      In you Lord I still abide, my faith is not shaken
And like the flowers that will bloom again from now, not long
      Bring back blessings into my life, God reward me with new
      awakenings

      In Christ's namesake, Amen

CHAPTER TWENTY TWO

THE NEW TEMPLE IS MADE CLEAN

May 29, 1987

I wrote this vision on June 1, 1987. God sent me a vision which made it clear to me the meaning of the black bull and the blood from the body of the bull. The chosen seven people were taken from the cliff at the edge of heaven. They were just barely into heaven. Many angels lifted the ground on which they stood. It was twenty feet square. The angels placed the ground onto the top of four pillars that were white, fluted and had scroll work at the top. The people went to their knees and prayed that they would be kept safe from evil. I picked up the head of the bull and used it to smear blood all over the pillars. I started at the left front pillar and smeared blood on it. I said, "With this you are sanctified in God forever." Then the right rear column was smeared with blood. I said, "Now the earth is cleansed from evil forever in this generation, but it will return to try our new seed." And as I smeared blood on the left rear column, the voices of many millions of angels sang out, "We have destroyed the old temple for it was unclean and now we have the sanctified altar for a new temple. It is most holy. Keep it clean and do not defile it with evil." God then lifted the altar with those saved into heaven. I could see the platform move up and slowly rotate. It disappeared into paradise into the distance.

Next God spoke to me and said, "You will be guardian of our new temple. Protect it well." I could see a new temple descend and rotate slowly from heaven. God placed it on a large hill and the altar squarely on the columns I had smeared with the blood. He placed great ferocious lions at each corner at the base of the steps to protect it from evil.

He said to me, "You my guardian must be vigilant and keep this place holy. Let this place be an example of righteousness so that sinners may know what I mean by righteousness. Light the lamp of mercy and compassion and show them the way to the light of God, the Father of Salvation. Remember Jesus will save them from their blindness. You will only show them to my Son with your lamp. And surely all their days that follow will be good. They will open their hearts to the spirit and know the meaning of love. Love endures. It outshines everything. The lamp post of love is God. In the valley of the shadow of death look unto God and the *messenger* to light the way. Do not look behind or to the sides, but forward to the light."

The vision ended.

These words from God resemble the Lord's Prayer. I am elated to know that these words from God in the form of the Lord's Prayer have been in the Bible for a long time.

CHAPTER TWENTY THREE

GOD SENDS AN ANGEL TO EXPLAIN THE TEMPLE OF GOD AND MY ROLE AT THE TEMPLE

Last week of November, 1987

I wrote this in December, 1987. This vision came to me and I wrote this the next week.

God has given to me through the angels and visions a greater understanding of the word of God and how it will be after this life. However, you should not look to me as a person who knows all there is to know about these truths. Only God knows all the truths and it is also his role to judge people and not mine. With great faith and compassion I see more of his wisdom than many others. You may ask me how it will be after I or you die. You will have a body but it will not be like your earthly physical body. There are pains and burdens you feel here on this world. I say to you that when God lifts you up to heaven, it will be as if you fly on wings and soar all about the heavens and universe. You will not feel pain, but remorse for those in need. Be not afraid for it is good. It is natural to fear the unknown, but be not so concerned with death and rebirth. Did you fret and worry when you entered this world from your mother's womb. No you did not. You breathed the air of life free from worry. In heaven you will breathe the life from love. The spirit of God is good.

Now God has told me this. "Great has been his anger to the children of Israel. They did condemn and kill his only son here on earth." But the Lord also says, "Do not punish my promised children of Israel. Judgment is mine. The Lord will determine who is to be taken up with the angels and who will be cast down. If you are righteous, you will feel remorse and mercy for the people who did not and do not accept the son. Now my anger is quiet and in this year of 1987 my word rains down equally on all. From this time on there will be a new age and there will be a new temple." God has said, "I will make an altar on earth for justice, truth and mercy. No longer will the way of the apostles of Jesus be the only way. New words and messages from our Lord will rain down upon the world." This I speak not from my own knowledge, but God has told me this.

If it should appear or be so that I exalt myself above our Lord Jesus then you have not properly interpreted the message. If you accept my message, then you accept our Lord Jesus and this means you accept our Father. If my words be other than from our Lord and Father, then do not listen, but turn away from them instead. To listen to the evil one, the false prophet, or anyone who follows them means darkness and death. In our Lord and Father is light and everlasting life. God has given the details of the construction of his new temple for this new age. This is given for people who are righteous to build.

And the Lord says to me concerning the new age and the temple, "All those who contribute their time, funds and work to build this new temple, I will bless them with rewards beyond their imagination. Those who come to my temple and sacrifice at my altar I will listen and answer them. To sacrifice means to turn your sins over to God. If you turn your life over to God, then should he accept you and have a special task for you, you will be his disciple. It means you leave your sins with God. Be sincere of heart and bring your very soul to him for God knows your true mind and intentions." You can not lie to God without his knowing it.

The instructions to build a new temple were given to me in a number of visions. God will not relieve me from this task until it is written down and given to the people. God has shown me in a vision this temple and he has explained the ages of mankind. God said, "The central part of the temple shall be a place of worship. I am not concerned with the overall dimensions of the temple. But that building that houses my altar shall be white all about and it shall be a most holy place. It will be more than a church or synagogue. At the center of the building and in the center of the dome shall be an altar. It shall be twenty by twenty feet wide and be of white marble. You may ask why this altar is to be twenty by twenty." The answer is sayeth God, "There are three ages of my reign over mankind. The first age is that age in which Moses brought forth my word and the world knew my power, my laws and my mercy. This was the age of God's law given to the people by Moses. The second age is that in which my Son, the Branch of God brought forth salvation and the Holy Spirit with love and mercy into the world. The people of the world have worshiped our Lord through his Laws and his Son. The third age is that for which the temple is built. This is the age where new prophets will bring forth words from God into the world not replacing the old prophecies and Scripture but to fulfill them and tell of new miracles not yet seen. My word, the word of God will rain down on the world as a heavy down pour in a rain storm and there will be many miracles."

Then God's angels told me, "The person, who is writing these words, Dennis Wayne Schroll, has been chosen by God to be the *first prophet of the new age*. He will announce the coming of more prophets to make new miracles and bring forth more words of faith from our Lord." Then the Lord sent an angel to me and the Book was revealed to me where it says God has promised the new temple and new prophecies in the existing *Scriptures*. The angel continued, "For just as the dove brought the leaf of the olive tree back to Noah so shall the Lord bring back the new age to the world. All that look unto our Lord shall have peace and everlasting life and they shall not perish into the sea of sin." Now the angel showed me in the Good Book of the Lord, "The Lord created the world in seven days and nights and seven is most holy. Three ages by seven holy days is twenty one. But from this our Lord will subtract one sacrifice that our Christ made. Christ died for your sins so the breadth of your sacrifice is twenty-one minus one or twenty. Twenty by twenty is most holy and it shall be the Holy of Holies throughout the new age." Then the angel showed me a new vision. In this age God says, "My Son shall return near its end and gather his flock. He shall come to this temple to reign as King of Kings and Priest of Priests. His judgment shall be fair."

The angels led me down the hallway of his Father's temple and I could see small chapels on the sides. The angel led me into the altar room and pointed to the altar. He showed me that the top of the altar will be the place upon which a golden hemispherical urn or bowl three feet in diameter be placed at the center. The angel said, "It will have two rod shaped handles at opposite sides that are seven inches wide and four inches above the rim. God said, "In this bowl shall you place your sacrifices. The altar surface shall be seven inches thick and olive branches and leaves shall adorn all about the edge. It shall not necessarily be solid stone but it should be of stable construction and the altar shall have the appearance of the seven inch thick dimension. This means the interior of the altar surface, under the upper surface, may be hollow to reduce weight to the columns. Set the altar on top of the four pillars, one at each corner. Each pillar shall look to hold the altar to a height suitable for viewing when kneeling, sacrificing sins and praying to our Lord. They will be fluted and scrolls shall be draped over their tops to remind all of the Book of Life."

The angel said, "That Book of Life is that Book into which each person's name is written in heaven. It is that book from which our Lord God reads on the end of a person's life. From the golden hall of records the good deeds are weighed. The sins and righteous deeds are placed on a scale and the righteous deeds should outweigh the sins. Below the surface of the altar place a rosewood chest with brass about the corners and edges. This shall be built with prayers. Set this chest on a table of low height draped with a red linen cloth. The chest shall measure four feet wide by three feet deep by two feet high. This chest will represent a person's reward for the sacrifices that they make." The angel said, "This is the vision of the temple and it's Holy of Holies, the altar, as it is in heaven it shall be built on earth."

The angel of God then said to me. "Do not sacrifice your animals or possessions or money. These are earthly things. If you give this, do it for others benefit and construction of the temple. That is an act of righteousness and charity. But instead bring to me your willingness for service. I ask that you sacrifice your sins in Jesus namesake. Be a good and righteous person. Do so and I will accept you gladly. Bring your faith and trust and service for your Lord. Serve with righteousness. If you turn your back on our Lord when you leave his temple, then God will turn his back on you. God will not wish damnation on you, but you may be without miracles in your life. Bring your sins, leave them and walk out a new person, clothed with faith willingness to serve your Lord." Then the angel showed me God's Temple in heaven again and he said, "Set our Lord's altar and treasures on a platform three steps above the floor so it will be in the third age of our Lord. Place a lightly stained oak railing with spindles on the perimeter of the top floor that is under the altar. It shall encircle the altar and treasures. Provide red carpet on the first and second steps with red cushions on the second step for kneeling in prayer at our Lord's altar so he may better listen to his children. Also, provide red carpet on the floor all about this part of the temple that houses the altar. The floor of the altar shall be white marble for it is most holy. As each part of God's church is built and constructed make prayers for many persons to visit our Lord for his compassion is great."

Then the angel led me by my hand throughout the rest of the temple as it is in heaven. We walked all about so that is would be impressed into my mind and not forgotten. The angel of God then said, "This is God's Temple as it looks in heaven. Tell the world so they may build our Lord's temple on the world for our Lord wants to be close to his children. The south side shall be the foot and the primary entrance to

My Temple. Therefore on the south side of the altar place the words, 'Holy of Holies.' On the north side place the words, 'God is Love, Place no others before me'. On the east side place the words, 'Love thy self and love thy neighbor but most of all love thy Lord.' On the west side place the words, 'Jesus is Lord, in his name is salvation.' On the floor to the east and west sides of the altar but facing south place statues and images, one on each side, of the cherubim angels to guard our Lord's altar from evil. The cherubim angels' statues and images are only material objects but they represent to the people that our Lord or God's throne is nearby the people. The cherubim bodies shall stand not higher than the altar, but their wings may extend above all the altar."

The angel of our Lord said to you, "That you may know my words said at this Temple and so that many may listen, provide seating and lighting. Lights shall shine straight down on all from above and most of all above the altar to show that the word of God rains down from heaven on all! The roof over the altar shall be a dome and it shall show a rainbow for the promise of the Lord and angels to guard the way to salvation. The background shall be blue as is the sky for our Lord does not want anyone to be shielded from his word."

Then the angel grabbed my arm and lifted me up high into the air to show me the entire temple as it appeared from a distance. The whole temple was in the shape of a cross. The angel of God said, "That as our Lord God looks down on the temple he wants to see the cross his Son died on. The doors to the temple shall be from each side, north, east, south and west. The doors at each entrance shall measure a total of twenty feet wide and seven feet high. Each door should be three or more feet wide by seven or more feet high and there shall be four or more doors. These doors may be split so they open separately from opposing hinges. There are four doors in all at each entrance. This is to remind you that twenty is the breadth of your sacrifice and seven is most holy. Place pillars with fluting and with scrolls on top from the top down each outside wall and at the entrances. The roof that radiates each direction from the altar room shall be a gable style and a triangle shaped pediment shall be located above each doorway. The triangle shall represent the Father, the Son and the Holy Ghost. The Holy Ghost is at the bottom of the triangle which supports our Lord and Son and it comes from the earth to above in heaven. The right side of the triangle represents our Lord Jesus who is seated at the right side of our Lord God and the left side represents our Lord God. None are above or below each other but all are strong with a triangle."

I can see that the Temple of God is located near dark colored mountains. The Temple of God is not in the mountains but on a large hill or mound miles from the mountains. I cannot say where this is as the Lord did not reveal this to me. Also he did not preclude more than one of these temples but he did not say anything about this. He does imply there is only one temple that Christ shall rule from. It is stated in many places in the Bible that God's Temple for the return of Jesus will be built in Israel.

And the angel of God continued to say, "Place patios at each side of the wings of the temple that extend from the dome which is at the center of the cross shaped building which covers the altar. The gable roof shall overhang the sides of the building to act as shelter for the patios. Pillars shall be placed at the perimeter of these patios and they shall hold the roof. The sides of the building that extend from the dome covered place shall have large windows with large panes included to let in much light. Place these between each chapel on the inside. The floor of the north building shall be alternating black and white squares that are each three feet square for the black and white horsemen that patrol the north. The floor of the south building which is the base of the cross shall be white three feet squares for this is the most holy entrance. The floor shall be red three feet squares on the east and west buildings that are the arms of the cross for the red horsemen that patrol all about the earth. The floor of the patio about the north, east, south and west wings shall be three feet square dapple gray for the pain and agony of the dapple gray horsemen that patrols the sins in the world. Agony and grief follow this horseman and his horse for it is written that sin shall be outside the Lord's temple and in the world. Any sin that is brought inside the temple shall be turned over to God and left at his altar."

An angel of God continued to say, "This temple shall be the temple of our Lord. For it is written that the branch of Jesse shall have his temple. He shall rule therein. He shall be priest on the throne of this temple and he shall bring much peace into the world. When Jesus our Savior returns, He shall reside in this temple. From here he shall call up his own and gather his flock. If you are not at the temple when he comes, do not worry for he will beckon you to come." In conclusion the angel of God then said to me, "Seven more major prophets will follow he who will write down these words and tell prophecies of the wisdom of our Lord. The words God gave to me and the words of the future prophets shall be contained in this temple for all who seek to pray and sacrifice at the Holy of Holies. My doors are open to you. Seek and you shall find." Amen

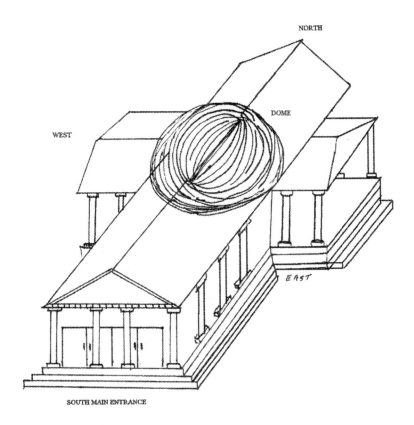

General Description of the Temple of God
(Note: the overall size and number of columns is optional)

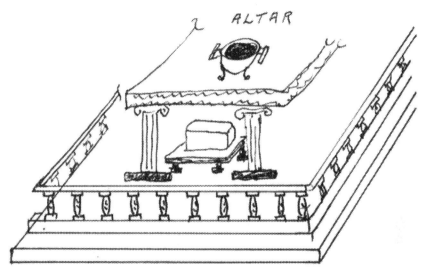

The Temple of God Altar,
(Note: The number of spindles and step dimensions are optional)

CHAPTER TWENTY FOUR

A MESSAGE FROM OUR LORD, THE HOLY OF HOLIES

June 11, 1987

This is a message to church leaders, leaders of all countries of the world and others who are concerned. God has told me to tell you all about his intentions. You must listen to be saved by our Lord to escape death and destruction on the return of Jesus. I wrote this message immediately after the vision from God on June 11, 1987.

God had said to me to tell all, "Greetings, listen to my words. I have sent to you a *messenger* to give the Good News. Before he was born I knew him. Listen to him and my judgment will bring you rewards you cannot even imagine. Dennis Wayne Schroll has been given the instrument of repentance. I say to you repent now. Humble yourself before your Lord. Listen to my *messenger* and he will show you the way to my kingdom."

I want to tell you that God looked into his temple. God said, "It is empty. There is no one at my altar. But look at the dust of sin. There are footsteps from the front door up to the altar. I sent my prophets and apostles and saints to bring light into the world and some did find their way to my altar. Look at the altar; they took the blood of

162

Christ. It is good. Why did they not leave a sacrifice to me? They left me many promises but still the altar is empty. Under my altar is my promise. The rewards I promised to you. When you fulfill your promises to me, I will open my treasure and reward you many times over." The Lord says, "Remember to repent now, and you will receive many rewards beyond your imagination. You cannot conceive how great this will be." This is a prophecy for the future when the Temple of God has been built and persons use the temple to worship God.

A prayer to God in Jesus Christ.

> I, the *messenger*, send a prayer for all humanity, "My Heavenly Father, you could bring down your voice from heaven for all to hear your commandments for you created the heavens and earth and all that is about the earth. Still you chose me, a person with sin to be your *messenger*. I am not worthy to clean your feet, Oh Lord. Why do you wish me to bring your words to the world? They may not listen, Oh Lord. Will you then bring down your anger on them? How can so many people change their ways? They seem to be content with their path of self-destruction. If good is stronger than evil, Oh Lord, then why is evil everywhere I look. They all have hardened their hearts. Few seem to have mercy for others, especially the weaker and those in need. It is my prayer that their hearts will be softened and become open to your everlasting mercy. Amen"

Lord, you showed me your temple and you said, "It is empty! Where are my children?" Then you showed me a place of great sin and you said, "Here they are. They are content with their own self-destruction. My temple is empty." Lord you want me to say, "Repent for the time is near. Lord you say that you are angry. My altar has no sacrifices on it. It has only empty promises." But I say unto you Oh Lord that a few have come to your altar in the old temple. I know this and I have seen this. I prayed Oh Lord and you told me, "Our Lord will not bring death and destruction to this generation as foretold earlier. I will bring mercy and compassion. This is under the condition that many begin to repent and turn to our Lord." God has said, "Because my *messenger* had asked for forgiveness for all humanity, I will not come with judgment in this generation." God said to me, "You must tell all to repent. They must bring sacrifices of their sins with their unbending faith. Worship me and not your worldly pursuits. Turn you sins over to God and leave your sacrifices of sin at the Temple of God's altar. Mercy is for all who seek, but those who turn to our Lord must repent. Do not worship those worldly things like money and power. Seek those good things that are in heaven."

The Lord sayeth, "To my *messenger* I tell you good news. Death and destruction will not come in this generation because you have been saved by the strong faith of a few. But I say unto you that you must cast aside your sins and repent or you will surely die. In sin there is only death and eternal damnation. In the Father, the Son and the Holy Ghost there is everlasting life."

God said in conclusion, "And when you, Dennis, begin to sweep away the dust of the sins of all the people of the world in my temple. I will cause the light from my prophets, saints and apostles to fall to the earth." In the third age, God's light and miracles will rain down upon the world as a downpour in a great thunderstorm. Heed the light and be happy for the miracles. Heaven waits for you if you ask for repentance."

This will fulfill the prophecy given in Hosea 6:1-3 in the 8th century BC more than 2 thousand and seven hundred years ago.

[1]*Come, and let us return unto the LORD: for he hath torn, and he will heal us; he hath smitten, and he will bind us up.*

[2]*After two days will he revive us: in the third day he will raise us up, and we shall live in his sight.*

³Then shall we know, if we follow on to know the LORD: his going forth is prepared as the morning; and he shall come unto us as the rain, as the latter and former rain unto the earth

I said, "Lord, I have been trying to sweep the dust away with my words. Those with hardened hearts contaminate the many innocents that are beginning to listen to your words. You tell me to love all those including those who sin greatly and those of faith. As soon as I sweep away the dust of sin those many who are seeking the truth, those with harden hearts blow back the dust in their zeal to harm the innocents. Lord what must I do to reach those who seek to harm others? I pray that you will soon answer me because I am but one among millions of souls in this world. I do not know if I have lit any candles of faith but I am trying with love in my heart. I want very much to do as you say. My faith is exceedingly strong and I shall not waiver. I only ask for more guidance about dealing with those who follow Satan. Oh Lord reveal to me if I am doing your will."

I continued to say, "Oh Lord, I have heard your words and have found the way to reach the people. I will put down to written words the miracles you have shown me and what the angels and you have said to me. If the people have a chance to experience the visions and see the wonders of God as I have seen them and hear the words I have heard, then I think many of those hardened hearts will soften. Therefore, your guidance is to put a book together and provide it to all who seek. With your guidance Oh Lord, the word will reach many. Thank you, Oh Lord!"

CHAPTER TWENTY FIVE

THE PROPHECY OF THE MESSENGER IS FULFILLED

December, 1987

One evening while I was resting from a day of work at the office, the Lord sent me a glorious angel. The angel revealed to me that the wonderful days of my visions had been foretold many times and many years ago. The words from our Lord were spoken more than two thousand years ago as the coming of a *prophet*, who is the *messenger*, was foretold. This *prophet* would announce that he comes before one who is much greater than he. He is speaking of the return of our Lord Christ. The angel then revealed to me that seven more prophets will follow me. This prophet, Dennis Wayne Schroll is the *first prophet* and *messenger* of the new age that God has revealed. Also, the angel said that the new Temple of God with its altar, the Holy of Holies, is foretold in the Good Book (Bible). The angel then recited the Bible verses to me while in prayer. The angel desired that I not forget these versus so he told me of the books, chapters and verse numbers where I will find these prophecies. I immediately copied down the reference books, chapters and verses because there were many to know. I could not hope to remember all that was given to me.

I have included these verses in their entirely below. The verses that are underlined are those that the angel specifically pointed out to me showing how the prophecy will be fulfilled with my visions and visions of the temple for the return of Jesus. The angel showed that when the Temple of God is built, then the prophecy will be fulfilled sometime after this. Truly the temple that is your own body is God's greatest temple, but God wishes that his son have his own temple on his return to gather his followers. Also, at the end of this vision the angel wished to make it very clear to me that I, Dennis Wayne Schroll, am the *messenger* or the spirit of Elijah as was prophesized approximately two thousand and five hundred years ago. The real Elijah died over two thousand years ago, but I have been tutored by the spirit of Elijah and I am his student who speaks as he would speak. I am the *first prophet* of the new age and the most important *messenger* that people should look to find God's words. The angels have said that my coming has fulfilled many prophesies given in the Good Book (Bible). In the Good Book there is also many prophesies and of a new Temple of God, the return of Christ and the judgment time.

It is strange to me to note that no reference to John the Baptist has been made in any of my visions. I do not understand why his spirit has remained hidden to me, but God knows best. At the time of Jesus, John the Baptist was considered the spirit of Elijah that came before one much greater than he, who is Jesus, who is the Messiah. When asked by the Jewish priests, John the Baptist denied he was Elijah so they did not believe Jesus was the Messiah. God knows the answer to this puzzling issue so I wait on God to reveal to me one day about John the Baptist.

These are the Bible verses about the building of the new God's Temple and the rewards God offers to build the temple for Jesus Christ.

1 Corinthians 3:8-17 (King James Version)

"8Now he that planteth and he that watereth are one: and every man shall receive his own reward according to his own labour.

⁹For we are labourers together with God: ye are God's husbandry, ye are God's building.

¹⁰According to the grace of God which is given unto me, as a wise masterbuilder, I have laid the foundation, and another buildeth thereon. But let every man take heed how he buildeth thereupon.

¹¹For other foundation can no man lay than that is laid, which is Jesus Christ.

¹²Now if any man build upon this foundation gold, silver, precious stones, wood, hay, stubble;

¹³Every man's work shall be made manifest: for the day shall declare it, because it shall be revealed by fire; and the fire shall try every man's work of what sort it is.

¹⁴If any man's work abide which he hath built thereupon, he shall receive a reward.

¹⁵If any man's work shall be burned, he shall suffer loss: but he himself shall be saved; yet so as by fire.

¹⁶Know ye not that ye are the Temple of God, and that the Spirit of God dwelleth in you?

¹⁷If any man defile the Temple of God, him shall God destroy; for the Temple of God is holy, which temple ye are."

The Temple of God that should be built in the world that is for Jesus' returning is mentioned in the Bible verses below.

1 Corinthians 9:10-17 (King James Version)

"¹⁰Or saith he it altogether for our sakes? For our sakes, no doubt, this is written: that he that ploweth should plow in hope; and that he that thresheth in hope should be partaker of his hope.

¹¹If we have sown unto you spiritual things, is it a great thing if we shall reap your carnal things?

[12]If others be partakers of this power over you, are not we rather? Nevertheless we have not used this power; but suffer all things, lest we should hinder the gospel of Christ.

[13]Do ye not know that they which minister about holy things live of the things of the temple? and they which wait at the altar are partakers with the altar?

[14]Even so hath the Lord ordained that they which preach the gospel should live of the gospel.

[15]But I have used none of these things: neither have I written these things, that it should be so done unto me: for it were better for me to die, than that any man should make my glorying void.

[16]For though I preach the gospel, I have nothing to glory of: for necessity is laid upon me; yea, woe is unto me, if I preach not the gospel!

[17]For if I do this thing willingly, I have a reward: but if against my will, a dispensation of the gospel is committed unto me."

So God has chosen me, Dennis Wayne Schroll, to be his *messenger* as I found out near the end of the many visions that came to me. He has made it clear that he wishes me to tell the people of the world that many prophecies will be fulfilled. Also, God and his angels have revealed to me that seven more prophets will be chosen after me to tell of new wonders. All of these prophets will tell that Christ will return at the end of this new age. I cannot be certain that Christ returns near the end of this age but it was implied to me after the many things that were said. No heavenly person, angel or God has told me when Christ is to return. Additionally, that which is much more important is that God has spoken through his angels and given me somewhat detailed directions for those who follow his teachings to build a temple for the return of Jesus our Lord and Savior. So that all will know that this is the will of our Lord, the angels have told me this was foretold in the Bible as shown below (Malachi 3:1-5; 3:12-18; and 4:1-6; Zechariah 3:1-10; 4:1-14; 6:1-15; 8:1-23; 9:1-17; and 14:1-21).

Malachi 3:1-5 (King James Version)

"¹Behold, I will send my messenger, and he shall prepare the way before me: and the LORD, whom ye seek, shall suddenly come to his temple, even the messenger of the covenant, whom ye delight in: behold, he shall come, saith the LORD of hosts.

²But who may abide the day of his coming? and who shall stand when he appeareth? for he is like a refiner's fire, and like fullers' soap:

³And he shall sit as a refiner and purifier of silver: and he shall purify the sons of Levi, and purge them as gold and silver, that they may offer unto the LORD an offering in righteousness.

⁴Then shall the offering of Judah and Jerusalem be pleasant unto the LORD, as in the days of old, and as in former years.

⁵And I will come near to you to judgment; and I will be a swift witness against the sorcerers, and against the adulterers, and against false swearers, and against those that oppress the hireling in his wages, the widow, and the fatherless, and that turn aside the stranger from his right, and fear not me, saith the LORD of hosts."

Malachi 3:12-18 (King James Version)

¹²And all nations shall call you blessed: for ye shall be a delightsome land, saith the LORD of hosts.

¹³Your words have been stout against me, saith the LORD. Yet ye say, What have we spoken so much against thee?

¹⁴Ye have said, It is vain to serve God: and what profit is it that we have kept his ordinance, and that we have walked mournfully before the LORD of hosts?

¹⁵And now we call the proud happy; yea, they that work wickedness are set up; yea, they that tempt God are even delivered.

¹⁶Then they that feared the LORD spake often one to another: and the LORD hearkened, and heard it, and a book of remembrance was

written before him for them that feared the LORD, and that thought upon his name.

[17]And they shall be mine, saith the LORD of hosts, in that day when I make up my jewels; and I will spare them, as a man spareth his own son that serveth him.

[18]Then shall ye return, and discern between the righteous and the wicked, between him that serveth God and him that serveth him not.

Malachi 4:1-6 (King James Version)

Judgment and Covenant Renewal

"[1]For, behold, the day cometh, that shall burn as an oven; and all the proud, yea, and all that do wickedly, shall be stubble: and the day that cometh shall burn them up, saith the LORD of hosts, that it shall leave them neither root nor branch.

[2]But unto you that fear my name shall the Sun of righteousness arise with healing in his wings; and ye shall go forth, and grow up as calves of the stall.

[3]And ye shall tread down the wicked; for they shall be ashes under the soles of your feet in the day that I shall do this, saith the LORD of hosts.

[4]Remember ye the law of Moses my servant, which I commanded unto him in Horeb for all Israel, with the statutes and judgments.

[5]Behold, I will send you Elijah the prophet before the coming of the great and dreadful day of the LORD:

[6]And he shall turn the heart of the fathers to the children, and the heart of the children to their fathers, lest I come and smite the earth with a curse."

These Bible verses speak of the return of Christ and the future seven prophets.

Zechariah 3:1-10 (King James Version)

¹And he showed me Joshua the high priest standing before the angel of the LORD, and Satan standing at his right hand to resist him.

²And the LORD said unto Satan, The LORD rebuke thee, O Satan; even the LORD that hath chosen Jerusalem rebuke thee: is not this a brand plucked out of the fire?

³Now Joshua was clothed with filthy garments, and stood before the angel.

⁴And he answered and spake unto those that stood before him, saying, Take away the filthy garments from him. And unto him he said, Behold, I have caused thine iniquity to pass from thee, and I will clothe thee with change of raiment.

⁵And I said, Let them set a fair mitre upon his head. So they set a fair mitre upon his head, and clothed him with garments. And the angel of the LORD stood by.

⁶And the angel of the LORD protested unto Joshua, saying,

⁷Thus saith the LORD of hosts; If thou wilt walk in my ways, and if thou wilt keep my charge, then thou shalt also judge my house, and shalt also keep my courts, and I will give thee places to walk among these that stand by.

⁸Hear now, O Joshua the high priest, thou, and thy fellows that sit before thee: for they are men wondered at: for, behold, I will bring forth my servant the BRANCH.

⁹For behold the stone that I have laid before Joshua; upon one stone shall be seven eyes: behold, I will engrave the graving thereof, saith the LORD of hosts, and I will remove the iniquity of that land in one day.

¹⁰In that day, saith the LORD of hosts, shall ye call every man his neighbour under the vine and under the fig tree.

This Bible verse speaks of the return of Jesus Christ and the future seven prophets before him.

Zechariah 4:1-14 (King James Version)

"¹And the angel that talked with me came again, and waked me, as a man that is wakened out of his sleep.

²And said unto me, What seest thou? And I said, I have looked, and behold a candlestick all of gold, with a bowl upon the top of it, and his seven lamps thereon, and seven pipes to the seven lamps, which are upon the top thereof:

³And two olive trees by it, one upon the right side of the bowl, and the other upon the left side thereof.

⁴So I answered and spake to the angel that talked with me, saying, What are these, my lord?

⁵Then the angel that talked with me answered and said unto me, Knowest thou not what these be? And I said, No, my lord.

⁶Then he answered and spake unto me, saying, This is the word of the LORD unto Zerubbabel, saying, Not by might, nor by power, but by my spirit, saith the LORD of hosts.

⁷Who art thou, O great mountain? before Zerubbabel thou shalt become a plain: and he shall bring forth the headstone thereof with shoutings, crying, Grace, grace unto it.

⁸Moreover the word of the LORD came unto me, saying,

⁹The hands of Zerubbabel have laid the foundation of this house; his hands shall also finish it; and thou shalt know that the LORD of hosts hath sent me unto you.

¹⁰For who hath despised the day of small things? for they shall rejoice, and shall see the plummet in the hand of Zerubbabel with those seven; they are the eyes of the LORD, which run to and fro through the whole earth.

¹¹Then answered I, and said unto him, What are these two olive trees upon the right side of the candlestick and upon the left side thereof?

¹²And I answered again, and said unto him, What be these two olive branches which through the two golden pipes empty the golden oil out of themselves?

¹³And he answered me and said, Knowest thou not what these be? And I said, No, my lord."

¹⁴Then said he, These are the two anointed ones, that stand by the LORD of the whole earth.

These Bible verses speak of the return of Jesus Christ and the future seven prophets before him.

Zechariah 6:1-15 (King James Version)

"¹And I turned, and lifted up mine eyes, and looked, and, behold, there came four chariots out from between two mountains; and the mountains were mountains of brass.

²In the first chariot were red horses; and in the second chariot black horses;

³And in the third chariot white horses; and in the fourth chariot grisled and bay horses.

⁴Then I answered and said unto the angel that talked with me, What are these, my lord?

⁵And the angel answered and said unto me, These are the four spirits of the heavens, which go forth from standing before the LORD of all the earth.

⁶The black horses which are therein go forth into the north country; and the white go forth after them; and the grisled go forth toward the south country.

⁷And the bay went forth, and sought to go that they might walk to and fro through the earth: and he said, Get you hence, walk to and fro through the earth. So they walked to and fro through the earth.

⁸Then cried he upon me, and spake unto me, saying, Behold, these that go toward the north country have quieted my spirit in the north country.

⁹And the word of the LORD came unto me, saying,

¹⁰Take of them of the captivity, even of Heldai, of Tobijah, and of Jedaiah, which are come from Babylon, and come thou the same day, and go into the house of Josiah the son of Zephaniah;

¹¹Then take silver and gold, and make crowns, and set them upon the head of Joshua the son of Josedech, the high priest;

¹²And speak unto him, saying, Thus speaketh the LORD of hosts, saying, Behold the man whose name is The BRANCH; and he shall grow up out of his place, and he shall build the temple of the LORD:

¹³Even he shall build the temple of the LORD; and he shall bear the glory, and shall sit and rule upon his throne; and he shall be a priest upon his throne: and the counsel of peace shall be between them both.

¹⁴And the crowns shall be to Helem, and to Tobijah, and to Jedaiah, and to Hen the son of Zephaniah, for a memorial in the temple of the LORD.

¹⁵And they that are far off shall come and build in the temple of the LORD, and ye shall know that the LORD of hosts hath sent me unto you. And this shall come to pass, if ye will diligently obey the voice of the LORD your God."

These Bible verses speak of Christ returning and ruling from the new Temple of God on the holy mountain. These versus also speak of the new prophets in this age, the third age of God.

Zechariah 8:1-23 (King James Version)

The LORD Promises to Bless Jerusalem

"¹Again the word of the LORD of hosts came to me, saying,

²Thus saith the LORD of hosts; I was jealous for Zion with great jealousy, and I was jealous for her with great fury.

³Thus saith the LORD; I am returned unto Zion, and will dwell in the midst of Jerusalem: and Jerusalem shall be called a city of truth; and the mountain of the LORD of hosts the holy mountain.

⁴Thus saith the LORD of hosts; There shall yet old men and old women dwell in the streets of Jerusalem, and every man with his staff in his hand for every age.

⁵And the streets of the city shall be full of boys and girls playing in the streets thereof.

⁶Thus saith the LORD of hosts; If it be marvellous in the eyes of the remnant of this people in these days, should it also be marvellous in mine eyes? saith the LORD of hosts.

⁷Thus saith the LORD of hosts; Behold, I will save my people from the east country, and from the west country;

⁸And I will bring them, and they shall dwell in the midst of Jerusalem: and they shall be my people, and I will be their God, in truth and in righteousness.

⁹Thus saith the LORD of hosts; Let your hands be strong, ye that hear in these days these words by the mouth of the prophets, which were in the day that the foundation of the house of the LORD of hosts was laid, that the temple might be built.

^{10}For before these days there was no hire for man, nor any hire for beast; neither was there any peace to him that went out or came in because of the affliction: for I set all men every one against his neighbour.

^{11}But now I will not be unto the residue of this people as in the former days, saith the LORD of hosts.

^{12}For the seed shall be prosperous; the vine shall give her fruit, and the ground shall give her increase, and the heavens shall give their dew; and I will cause the remnant of this people to possess all these things.

^{13}And it shall come to pass, that as ye were a curse among the heathen, O house of Judah, and house of Israel; so will I save you, and ye shall be a blessing: fear not, but let your hands be strong.

^{14}For thus saith the LORD of hosts; As I thought to punish you, when your fathers provoked me to wrath, saith the LORD of hosts, and I repented not:

^{15}So again have I thought in these days to do well unto Jerusalem and to the house of Judah: fear ye not.

^{16}These are the things that ye shall do; Speak ye every man the truth to his neighbour; execute the judgment of truth and peace in your gates:

^{17}And let none of you imagine evil in your hearts against his neighbour; and love no false oath: for all these are things that I hate, saith the LORD.

^{18}And the word of the LORD of hosts came unto me, saying,

^{19}Thus saith the LORD of hosts; The fast of the fourth month, and the fast of the fifth, and the fast of the seventh, and the fast of the tenth, shall be to the house of Judah joy and gladness, and cheerful feasts; therefore love the truth and peace.

^{20}Thus saith the LORD of hosts; It shall yet come to pass, that there shall come people, and the inhabitants of many cities:

²¹And the inhabitants of one city shall go to another, saying, Let us go speedily to pray before the LORD, and to seek the LORD of hosts: I will go also.

²²Yea, many people and strong nations shall come to seek the LORD of hosts in Jerusalem, and to pray before the LORD.

²³Thus saith the LORD of hosts; In those days it shall come to pass, that ten men shall take hold out of all languages of the nations, even shall take hold of the skirt of him that is a Jew, saying, We will go with you: for we have heard that God is with you."

These verses speak of Christ ruling from the new Temple of God.

Zechariah 9:1-17

Judgment on Israel's Enemies

"¹The burden of the word of the LORD in the land of Hadrach, and Damascus shall be the rest thereof: when the eyes of man, as of all the tribes of Israel, shall be toward the LORD.

²And Hamath also shall border thereby; Tyrus, and Zidon, though it be very wise.

³And Tyrus did build herself a strong hold, and heaped up silver as the dust, and fine gold as the mire of the streets.

⁴Behold, the LORD will cast her out, and he will smite her power in the sea; and she shall be devoured with fire.

⁵Ashkelon shall see it, and fear; Gaza also shall see it, and be very sorrowful, and Ekron; for her expectation shall be ashamed; and the king shall perish from Gaza, and Ashkelon shall not be inhabited.

⁶And a bastard shall dwell in Ashdod, and I will cut off the pride of the Philistines.

⁷And I will take away his blood out of his mouth, and his abominations from between his teeth: but he that remaineth, even he, shall be for our God, and he shall be as a governor in Judah, and Ekron as a Jebusite.

⁸And I will encamp about mine house because of the army, because of him that passeth by, and because of him that returneth: and no oppressor shall pass through them any more: for now have I seen with mine eyes.

⁹Rejoice greatly, O daughter of Zion; shout, O daughter of Jerusalem: behold, thy King cometh unto thee: he is just, and having salvation; lowly, and riding upon an ass, and upon a colt the foal of an ass.

¹⁰And I will cut off the chariot from Ephraim, and the horse from Jerusalem, and the battle bow shall be cut off: and he shall speak peace unto the heathen: and his dominion shall be from sea even to sea, and from the river even to the ends of the earth.

¹¹As for thee also, by the blood of thy covenant I have sent forth thy prisoners out of the pit wherein is no water.

¹²Turn you to the strong hold, ye prisoners of hope: even to day do I declare that I will render double unto thee;

¹³When I have bent Judah for me, filled the bow with Ephraim, and raised up thy sons, O Zion, against thy sons, O Greece, and made thee as the sword of a mighty man.

<u>¹⁴And the LORD shall be seen over them, and his arrow shall go forth as the lightning: and the LORD God shall blow the trumpet, and shall go with whirlwinds of the south.</u>

¹⁵The LORD of hosts shall defend them; and they shall devour, and subdue with sling stones; and they shall drink, and make a noise as through wine; and they shall be filled like bowls, and as the corners of the altar.

¹⁶And the LORD their God shall save them in that day as the flock of his people: for they shall be as the stones of a crown, lifted up as an ensign upon his land.

[17]For how great is his goodness, and how great is his beauty! corn shall make the young men cheerful, and new wine the maids."

These Bible verses speak of the new Temple of God which Christ shall rule the world on his return and the final Judgment Days. The prophecy (Zechariah 14:20-21), of the golden hemispherical urn or bowl which the righteous shall sacrifice their sins at the altar of the Temple of God as told in this book, is fulfilled when the temple is constructed.

Zechariah 14:1-21

The LORD Comes and Reigns

"[1]Behold, the day of the LORD cometh, and thy spoil shall be divided in the midst of thee.

[2]For I will gather all nations against Jerusalem to battle; and the city shall be taken, and the houses rifled, and the women ravished; and half of the city shall go forth into captivity, and the residue of the people shall not be cut off from the city.

[3]Then shall the LORD go forth, and fight against those nations, as when he fought in the day of battle.

[4]And his feet shall stand in that day upon the mount of Olives, which is before Jerusalem on the east, and the mount of Olives shall cleave in the midst thereof toward the east and toward the west, and there shall be a very great valley; and half of the mountain shall remove toward the north, and half of it toward the south.

[5]And ye shall flee to the valley of the mountains; for the valley of the mountains shall reach unto Azal: yea, ye shall flee, like as ye fled from before the earthquake in the days of Uzziah king of Judah: and the LORD my God shall come, and all the saints with thee.

[6]And it shall come to pass in that day, that the light shall not be clear, nor dark:

⁷But it shall be one day which shall be known to the LORD, not day, nor night: but it shall come to pass, that at evening time it shall be light.

⁸And it shall be in that day, that living waters shall go out from Jerusalem; half of them toward the former sea, and half of them toward the hinder sea: in summer and in winter shall it be.

⁹And the LORD shall be king over all the earth: in that day shall there be one LORD, and his name one.

¹⁰All the land shall be turned as a plain from Geba to Rimmon south of Jerusalem: and it shall be lifted up, and inhabited in her place, from Benjamin's gate unto the place of the first gate, unto the corner gate, and from the tower of Hananeel unto the king's winepresses.

¹¹And men shall dwell in it, and there shall be no more utter destruction; but Jerusalem shall be safely inhabited.

¹²And this shall be the plague wherewith the LORD will smite all the people that have fought against Jerusalem; Their flesh shall consume away while they stand upon their feet, and their eyes shall consume away in their holes, and their tongue shall consume away in their mouth.

¹³And it shall come to pass in that day, that a great tumult from the LORD shall be among them; and they shall lay hold every one on the hand of his neighbour, and his hand shall rise up against the hand of his neighbour.

¹⁴And Judah also shall fight at Jerusalem; and the wealth of all the heathen round about shall be gathered together, gold, and silver, and apparel, in great abundance.

¹⁵And so shall be the plague of the horse, of the mule, of the camel, and of the ass, and of all the beasts that shall be in these tents, as this plague.

¹⁶And it shall come to pass, that every one that is left of all the nations which came against Jerusalem shall even go up from year to year to worship the King, the LORD of hosts, and to keep the feast of tabernacles.

¹⁷And it shall be, that whoso will not come up of all the families of the earth unto Jerusalem to worship the King, the LORD of hosts, even upon them shall be no rain.

¹⁸And if the family of Egypt go not up, and come not, that have no rain; there shall be the plague, wherewith the LORD will smite the heathen that come not up to keep the feast of tabernacles.

¹⁹This shall be the punishment of Egypt, and the punishment of all nations that come not up to keep the feast of tabernacles.

²⁰In that day shall there be upon the bells of the horses, HOLINESS UNTO THE LORD; and the pots in the LORD's house shall be like the bowls before the altar.

²¹Yea, every pot in Jerusalem and in Judah shall be holiness unto the LORD of hosts: and all they that sacrifice shall come and take of them, and seethe therein: and in that day there shall be no more the Canaanite in the house of the LORD of hosts."

I realize that God has given detailed instructions for the building of his temple. He has told this to his prophets several thousand years ago. As far as I know this temple was never built. None of the angels mentioned this when telling me about the new Temple of God that they wish to be built here in the world. I wonder how God's people could have such harden hearts to the wishes of our Lord. God does not ask for things that are just for God alone. Those things like the building of his temple are for mankind and these instructions will increase the health and welfare of peoples in this world. Why does God so often ask that men and women give up their sins to God and Christ? This is the improvement of men and women and not necessarily God. God will be happy when we give up our sins and sad when we do not. It is mankind that suffers if their sins that are held close to their hearts are not given to God. God will not suffer.

CHAPTER TWENTY SIX

THE VOICE OF THE MESSENGER, BRING YOUR SACRIFICES TO THE ALTAR

First week of June, 1987

I wrote this on June 14, 1987. Does God send the strength of armies and their mighty power to say his words and then enforce them with the strength of his will? He does have that strength but, no, he uses his great wisdom for the benefit of his children for he loves them greatly. Those evil kings and rulers of countries in this world do send the might of their armies and enforce their words. They have taken sides with Satan.

My strength is in my covenant with our gentle Lord. He speaks to me because he has seen that my compassion and mercy for all is good. I am with God. The blind, the deaf, those wanting from grief, all races of peoples of the earth, those with burdens too great in their hearts to bear, the righteous, the sinners and any who seek out Lord's mercy will receive it from God. I, who am a servant of our Lord who is God, will help bring them to God so they may receive the loving salvation from God and not evil. God has said to me; go out into the world with a heart that is soft. Let your tears of loving compassion be there for all to see so that they may know the power of gentleness, the power of kindness and the power of mercy.

Lord, you have the golden scales of justice so help me weigh the gentleness, kindness and mercy of others. Some I may find wanting, Oh Lord. They seem to be foolish in their great knowledge. They knew what your words said. They could repeat those words and boast their knowledge for all the world to hear. But Lord they did not have your gentle ways in their hearts. They looked at others and said they know more about God than others do. They say, "I am more righteous." God I think you will agree with me when I say, "Shame on them." Lord, you can put their hearts on the golden scale of justice you gave me and you will find them wanting. Your weights of gentleness Oh Lord, they do tip the scales towards heaven and away from their worldly and selfish ways. Lord, they may say to others that they know you, but they do not. They do not understand what the fruit of gentleness means.

Others said they knew what you wanted so they would find favor in your eyes. Lord, they look up at you and say, "See how kind I am." I went to church and put my tokens in the tray. On the next day they went out and sinned against their brothers and sisters and took from them unjustly. I say to them, "Are you so smart that you think the Lord looks at you on Sunday and closes his eyes the rest of the week? How foolish you are. The Lord created you and the ground on which you walk. Do you think he is blind to your harsh ways when you want him to be? No, he looks always to see what his children are doing. The Lord is kind but he is not blind." Lord, I took the golden scales of justice and it tipped to you and your kindness from heaven. The scales did not tip to the harsh worldly ways of those foolish men. These men are blind for they think there is power in cruel ways and kindness is weakness. When they pass through judgment they will be most surprised to see that their cruel ways burn as the chaff from the wheat and the seed of kindness passes right on through to you. Lord I know you will reach out for their kindness and hold it in your hand and examine it. You will say, "Give me your kind heart and I will return treasures to you beyond all you can imagine."

And Lord what of the mercies of those here. They read your words and say he wants me to be merciful. How nice. I will pat a child on the head or give some food to charity. But my Lord they do not understand. They do not put mercy in their hearts. Are their tears for the sinners? When you see and look at a sinner and reach out to them do you think how you may show the light of the Lord? Oh foolish men and women you do not. You look and think to yourselves I am better than you. I, the redeemer from God, say to you that surely you have no mercy in your heart if you do not have tears for the sinners. Turn away from your self righteousness. Repent, says the Lord. Oh Lord, you can put them on the golden scale of justice and it will tip to your heavenly mercy and away from their worldly self righteousness. Surely I say to you that when you pass through the fires of judgment, your self righteousness will burn like straw but your mercies will be like hard gemstones. See the power of mercy for your salvation. God wants your mercies. Sinners I ask that you turn your feelings to the weak, the hungry and the sinners for they need you. They are as babies in your arms. Pluck the dirt from their eyes, unstop their ears and take the shields of self righteousness from their hearts.

Now self righteousness is not so bad a sin, but it is the minor sins that lead to greater sins. Many minor sins led a person on the path to self destruction and greater sins. Oh Lord, I pray they turn those minor sins over to you for all sins are bad in your eyes. We will watch with mercy in our hearts that those people realize they have taken the wrong path and they change their ways. Oh Lord let us all pray for them to be better men, women and children.

I say to you, sinners, repent! I say to you again, repent! Take the chains from your heart. One day with God is better than any day in the darkness of sin. Be happy says our Lord, not wanting. You, who feel righteous and are smug, take the mud from your eyes. Clean the blindness from your hearts. Do not look into the Good Book and say God is in there. Foolish people, God is on his throne at the Holy Mountain. Do not look down to the pages and pray. Look up to God and shout, "Praise the Lord, we are saved!" Run into the streets and dance for you are saved. Furthermore I say to you, "I am the word of God in the flesh. I tell you that when you truly see God, open him as a book and be refreshed. Read his pages and receive salvation. His spirit is like the cool and soothing drink that refreshes. Turn the pages of our Lord and be surprised at the rewards which await you. For before there was Grace and Christ, there was peace from God's spirit. Before a single word of God was put into a letter and passed down from one generation to the next, his gentleness, kindness and mercy refreshed those in need. And the Lord God said to me, "I am the Spirit. Those who drink from my fountain will be saved. Sin no more for the Lord loves you. And when the spirit is in you, gentleness, kindness, mercy and much more will be your fruit."

I, the *messenger* of God tell you these things so you may know where salvation truly lies.

God tells me that you bring only empty promises to his altar. Where are your sacrifices? The promises do not bring you blessings and rewards. The act will do that. Act on God's behalf. But, I say to you good deeds and righteousness for others are not enough. These deeds must be in God's name through our Lord Jesus Christ, for God and beside God. You must have strong faith in our Lord that he is real and he is salvation. Ask the Lord and if he wants your deeds, if he says yes, then act on his behalf. Christ died for you so that your sins would be cleansed. Ask Christ for salvation and then do this for him. Surely there is no greater act of compassion than to lay down your life for your friends, brothers and sisters of the world. Christ did this because he loves his people in this world. Remember to thank Christ for his act of compassion and pray to God with the friendship of Jesus Christ in mind.

Bring not your earthly possessions to the altar. God will breathe on them and turn them to dust. Bring not your dissatisfactions to the altar and dump them on God. He will put more burdens back on you for he waits for your sacrifices. Give God your sins and your dissatisfactions will no longer be on your mind. God says to me,

"Bring your spirit, your willingness and service to God. Place your heart on the altar and give it to God. Shake Christ's hand, turn around smiling and be happy for you will be a part of the family of Christ. Drink the blood of Christ, be refreshed by his body and leave your sacrifices to God." Do you think God will burden you with unending tasks and make your life weary? I say to you if he does, you will not be weary, you will be happy. Rejoice for you are a child of God and he is your Father. He will take care of you. You will be relieved of your burdens of sin. You will not want. If the world persecutes you because you speak for Christ, then be happy for then you know that Christ will speak for you on your Judgment Day. Amen

CHAPTER TWENTY SEVEN

MY VISION OF THE SERPENT

March, 1986

I wrote this down the day after the vision occurred. When I was living south of Tipp City, Ohio in 1986 I had another vision. While asleep one evening I heard a voice in my dream telling me to wake. It was a raspy voice that whispered in my mind's ear that I should look forward and downward at my legs. When I awoke, I felt great shock at seeing there was a yellowish green serpent wrapped about both of my legs. It was about three inches in diameter and its tail was on my upper left thigh. The end of the serpent coiled about my left leg down to my left foot. Its middle was crossed at my feet so that its coiling of the last one half of the serpent was about my right leg so that brought its head to my upper right thigh. Its head arched upward about 14 inches above my groin and it looked at me menacingly swaying to and fro from the left and to the right. It issued a forked tongue and had penetrating red eyes.

As I looked upon this terrible sight my heart pounded. "How can this be," was my first thought. "Was I dreaming?" I thought God had saved me before and so the evil serpent would not be after me anymore. The serpent spoke saying, "You are wrapped tightly in my clutches and you cannot escape. You are mine and nothing can take you from me. You will be held to my will. I will torment you with my power and then I will devour you. You are helpless." Its head lunged at my mouth as if to strike my face and I cried out to God, "My Lord Jesus I do not have the strength alone to fight off this evil serpent. Will you take me from its grip and save me? I love you my Lord Jesus. Do unto me as is your will for I know it will be good!" At that instant the serpent disappeared and my soul was filled with a deep peace and contentment.

Looking again at my legs a new vision appeared. It was a vine with leaves all wrapped around my legs. Then I heard a voice declare, "You have chosen the fruit of life over that of the power of the serpent. Bless you my son. You are wise. The fruit tastes better than power and you will receive its blessings." Then I could see all types and colors of fruits sprout from the vine and my heart was filled with much joy.

This had to be a vision from God for it stayed in my mind so crisp and clear not like a dream which quickly fades and is forgotten. A few days later the spirit revealed to me that this was the serpent that Moses had mounted a bronze replica in its image onto his staff. See Numbers 21:8-9, King James Version.

"8 Then the LORD said to Moses, "Make a fiery serpent (bronze replica), and set it on a pole; and it shall be that everyone who is bitten, when he looks at it, shall live." 9 So Moses made a bronze serpent, and put it on a pole; and so it was, if a serpent had bitten anyone (or sins in another sense), when he looked at the bronze serpent, he lived."

It is clear to me now that this vision was sent by God to test my faith in our Lord Jesus Christ. The pole (staff) was the cross Jesus died on. The serpent was not Christ, but Satan. The bronze serpent Moses lifted up was an image as Christ is today to stimulate faith by those bitten by Satan so that they can recover. Or, another way of stating this, is that just as I sin and exhibit pride, I am bitten by the serpent. When I look up at the pole (staff) and the bronze serpent I acknowledge that I have sinned. It is man's nature to sin. The pole (staff) should remind me that Christ died on the cross. I must profess my belief and faith in Christ to save me from the serpents or Satan and sin. For it is stated in John 3:13-21.

John 3:13-21 (King James Version (KJV))

"[13] And no man hath ascended up to heaven, but he that came down from heaven, even the Son of man which is in heaven.

[14] And as Moses lifted up the serpent in the wilderness; even so must the Son of man be lifted up:

[15] That whosoever believeth in him should not perish, but have eternal life.

[16] For God so loved the world, that he gave his only begotten Son, that whosoever believeth in him should not perish, but have everlasting life.

[17] For God sent not his Son into the world to condemn the world; but that the world through him might be saved.

[18] He that believeth on him is not condemned: but he that believeth not is condemned already, because he hath not believed in the name of the only begotten Son of God.

[19] And this is the condemnation, that light is come into the world, and men loved darkness rather than light, because their deeds were evil.

[20] For every one that doeth evil hateth the light, neither cometh to the light, lest his deeds should be reproved.

[21] But he that doeth truth cometh to the light, that his deeds may be made manifest, that they are wrought in God."

CHAPTER TWENTY EIGHT

CULTIVATE OUR SOULS WITH PRAYER, THE VISION OF THE FIELD OF MUD WITH POTHOLES

May 31, 1988

The souls of people are like fertile ground broken by the plow, ready for planting. If it rains just after the seed is sown, the force of the rain carries away the seed and it cannot be taken by the ground or by a person's soul. Evil is like the seed of the weeds that would take root in the soul and grow into worthless fields with no crop for yield. Wild fields in the plains of earth are not necessarily evil because it is God's wilderness. Weeds planted into the soul are as evil because the fruit of the spirit is absent. Weeds are like the sins of man and the seed of the intended crop is like the spirit from our Lord working its miracles with the soul.

If it rains after the good seed of the spirit is planted but not yet established, then the soil is washed about. Much seed will be lost. That depends on how severe the storm is. But, God promises that some good seed will always remain in the soil or man's soul. Children, it is far better to plow the weeds from the soul, allow much seed of the spirit to be planted, fertilize it with knowledge and cultivate it with prayer. This will ensure a good strong stand of crop able to weather the heaviest rain storm. God tells us that we have only to allow our fields to be cleared of weeds or sin so that the Grace of God may be sown into the soul. This allows the fruit of the Holy Spirit to flourish and grow within this person's soul.

God did show me a vision of a field of mud with many potholes. Much water is collected into the pot holes. God said, "See how the potholes collect water from above just as do the minds or souls of men and women collect the spirit. If the spirit is bad, the holes will be wretched and stink and nothing will be produced. When the rain is done, the soil will dry and the potholes will be only dry holes in a desert. The mind will be as a wasteland. This is as you would be to accept sin into your lives. If the spirit is good, then there will be a great difference. God and his angels will breathe life into the soul. The water in these potholes will refresh the good vines that grow just as a healthy spirit should grow. Much life will spring forth and this will multiply many times over. The spirit of God will be in the life and the life will be in the spirit of God. Peace will abound and all heaven and angels will be happy." God said, "This, I have promised you since Noah and the pact is sealed with the rainbow. Remember it is still a promise!" This, God said to me in a vision. God then said, "Write down these words for I wish everyone to remember my promise once again."

CHAPTER TWENTY NINE

THE SERMON AND MIRACLE OF SALVATION IN THE GARAGE

June 13, 1987

On June 10, 1987 we had an earthquake near Dayton, Ohio. I was living in Dayton, Ohio. This rarely happens here so it was of some note. It occurred to me after this earthquake happened that it was a message from God. Why is that? Just as I was ready to close the garage door the earthquake began. The quake rattled the ladders and items in my garage so much; it was as if God was protesting that the garage door not be closed.

This is related to my sermon about salvation in the garage. It was revealed to me that many people would have a better chance to find God and salvation in a garage than in a church. Why is that? A garage door opens big and wide for anyone. Some church doors seem to only open for those of the right class, the right color and the right behavior. Jesus said that he went out among the sinners because they needed him the most. Do our churches go out among the sinners? They seem sometimes to be more concerned with having those who seem already righteous. A garage will accept anyone. Your car will be serviced and made to run well again. Will the church service your heart and make your soul healthy again? They do not always seem as concerned with this as being righteous themselves and condemning the sinners. The sinners are blind. They do not see the light. God asks those of you who are righteous; if you indeed love God, will you please lead the sinners to righteousness.

That is the meaning of the sermon of the garage. You may more easily find salvation in a garage than in those churches that man has set up for his own self righteousness. If a church has opened its doors to all and they have self righteousness under control, then God will be pleased with them. Imagine the church is a garage and then the doors should be wide open to righteous and sinners alike. Jesus wants the sinners to repent their sinful ways and become servants of our Lord.

CHAPTER THIRTY

THE ARCHANGEL RAPHAEL VISITS MY BEDSIDE

1983

This was written on March 30, 1986. I have made a written record of my vision of the Archangel Raphael so that others may know of his presence in the Lord our Almighty God and his purposes in our lives.

It was in 1983 that I lie asleep in my bed in my house at Deer Cliff Run, Tipp City, Ohio. I was partially awake in the morning hours when it was light outside. I heard a voice calling me to "Awake and rise forward; you have a holy visitor from our most High!" Upon rising up and looking off the end of the foot of my bed and to the right there was a flood of white light that was most brilliant. This was unlike the sunlight which is yellow. This light was pure white. It shinned down through my ceiling of my bedroom so I thought it must be from heaven. I was awake to the real world and not in my spirit form.

As the light did dim somewhat I could see a brilliant golden halo of radiance shine about an angel. The angel was most glorious that was in the final course of slow descent down to the floor in front of me. The angel said in a voice that was soothing to my mind, "I am the Archangel Raphael! I have come! I am the angel of mercy and compassion. Give me your sick and I will heal them. Give me your blind and I will give them sight. God has empowered me to heal in our Lord's name. You have received my mercy. You were once in sickness and now you are healed. You were once in darkness and now you can see. Because you see me and believe, you have been given a task. Seek out those who are in great need and show them to our Lord. If they believe, they will be healed. Should you ever have need of me, call upon me and I will be there. Praise God our most Holy One in his Highest. Sing praises to all the angels and blessed are they who suffer for his namesake. They will see God and their hearts will be pure. Glory Hallelujah! Glory Hallelujah! Praise God!" It was then I realized that the Archangel Raphael was speaking to my mind and not my ears.

All the time the Archangel Raphael was speaking I was so stunned that my mouth would not move to talk or ask him anything. His presence was so great it was astounding just to behold him. He then stood there looking at me with deep blue eyes that seemed to twinkle with lights and a thin smile pursed his lips as if saying, I care for you and my heart bleeds when you suffer. Can I take on your pain and give you peace. He was there what seemed like many minutes without saying anything else. His image is burned into my mind so that I may never ever forget it.

He had golden yellow hair with a silken white headband that had golden embroidery on its edges. His hair dropped halfway to his shoulders and was slightly curled. He appeared to be about six feet and 6 inches tall but his feet did not show at the floor because his silken light blue robe covered his body down to the floor. His robe was over his arms also down to about his wrists. He held his arms outwards as if to embrace everyone and his hands were open. The robe was pleated like drapery and had golden embroidery about one inch from the edges with a square block pattern. This was much like that used by the ancient Greeks and Romans and is called the Greek key pattern. A large breast plate covered his chest and upper waist. It was white and had complicated golden embroidery all about it. The archangel had a light fair complexion without any blemishes that I could see. A light seemed to shine from within him. He had high cheekbones, a straight Greek or Roman nose, blonde eyebrows and medium sized ears that were close to his head. His wings were white and they arched upward several feet above his head and out to the side of his body. They went down to the floor and they looked like doves feathers. If I could paint the image from my mind, it would be translated to the canvas for all to see.

The Archangel Raphael then looked upward to heaven. I shook my head because I could hardly believe what my eyes were seeing. I had thought to get up and rush forward and embrace him for his holiness and kindness. I closed my eyes briefly and began to rise. Then he said, "I am the Archangel Raphael, behold I return to our most Holy God." A thunder clap sounded, a light shone down from heaven and he raised his arms and his wings outstretched from his body as to fly and he ascended to heaven. This was a most astounding sight to behold. It has never yet left my mind. I feel the presence of the Archangel Raphael most often to keep me feeling holy, close to God and free from sickness. The astounding thing about this visit is that it was to my earthly body and not my spirit. I realize then that none of my visions had ever been in my dreams. This was very real to me.

I did not realize until I wrote this book, but the Archangel Raphael freely gave me the power to heal people if I pray to him asking for his intervention and I also pray to Jesus. The ill person must have faith he or she will be healed. This is a wonderful gift which I have rarely used but I should take advantage of this more in the future and see if the gift is genuine.

CHAPTER THIRTY ONE

THE MIRACLE OF THE LIGHT
FROM HEAVEN

June 12, 1987

On the evening of June 12, 1987 as I drove home from work about 5:15 PM God showed me another miracle. The sun was behind a big dark cloud, but the golden white rays shone down not as if from the sun, but from heaven. This appeared as an announcement from God that the walls of the old church are thrown out and broken to dust. God's light and spirit will shine all about beginning on this day. On this day he will begin to build a new and better church. The actual material building will not happen until someone reading my words acts upon God's request. I cannot do this. Salvation will shine forth like the sun and God's mercy will reach many more. This begins a new age for God's new church.

The prophecy is fulfilled and today it begins just as it began several thousand years ago for Isaiah.

See Isaiah 45:4-13, 49:1-6; John 8:11-13, 9:4-6; 2 Corinthians 4:3-5; and Philippians 2:14-16

CHAPTER THIRTY TWO

VISION OF THE BABY FROM PARADISE

1983

I wrote this on November 12, 1987. One evening while I was living at Tipp City, Ohio, I was awakened from my sleep by what appeared to be the constant laughter and giggling of a child. This was strange because I knew there were no children in my home. I awoke and turned slowly to my right. There in front of me was the vision of a baby lying on a puffy white cloud. It was like a chubby two year old baby with small wings on its back just above its shoulder blades. The white feathered wings were only about the length of its short forearms or about 8 inches. The baby had a ruddy complexion with rosy plump cheeks and curly auburn or reddish hair. His little body was so plump; it appeared he would not be able to move. He had dark brown serious eyes and small hands and feet. He lay on his left side on a puffy cotton-like cloud about four feet long and five feet above the floor. He lay on his side with his right hand and arm out stretched as if reaching up to God. His left arm was under his head to prop it up and his elbow was below this. His right leg was also up in the air. He had a coy smug look on his face and he did not move at all or say anything.

I waited for a message from the vision of this baby and after what seemed like five minutes I shook my head vigorously as if in disbelief that it was really there. The baby still did not move. I then began to get up and move towards him to touch him. As I moved toward him the vision disintegrated in what seemed like patches disappearing before my eyes.

Chapter Thirty Three

Second Vision of the Baby in Paradise with an Angel

1983

A few days later after seeing the baby in paradise he came to me again. Some people refer to these babies in heaven as cherubs but this is not really correct. A cherub is the strong angel with the body of a lioness at the throne of God. In a fleeting moment of awakening in the darkness of the early morning my mind was insensitive to the reality of the entire world at first. I turned to my right and I beheld a wondrous sight. In a heavenly silver glow there were small tufts of a cloud with pillow-like bulbs over it all. It was tinted on the edges like an inward glow, a deep baby blue glow. This cloud seemed to be about 2 feet high and 3 to 4 feet long on the horizontal. The most startling sight of all was the figure of a small ruddy cheeked, curly red headed Baby in Paradise or a very young boy as it appeared to me. He was turned on his left side on one elbow facing directly towards me. On the lower side on the cloud was his bent left leg and the right leg was drawn up more to the body with it bent at the knee and thigh. It seemed to be a pose of motion of a baby in glee but there was no movement. It was as if it was a still picture of a white child with reddish skin tone and ruddy facial complexion. I do not remember any clothing about the child but a short bluish cloth could have been draped about indiscriminately but this was not easily determined.

I thought it was a dream at first, but then as I became awake I remember totally my surroundings and I was in a full alert wakefulness. The baby was still there. I waited with my breath held tight for a sign but to no avail. Then I just could not believe it. I shook my head and rubbed my eyes. Then I saw what looked like it had a glint in his eyes and he slowly faded away. The look in his eyes was as if he was trying to convey a message to me, but no message came to me. After it was over, I laid awake for awhile trying to figure what this was. It was not really a dream and then I thought it could be a hallucination. But, deep inside me, I knew it was a message or a premonition of something yet to come to me. That feeling was with me for a few days when the message did appear.

It was late one afternoon several days later when I was searching my soul and meditating on what to do with my future life. A large silver shaft of light thrust down from above and trumpets sounded joyous sounds as if it was an announcement yet to come. What did appear in front of me was an angel with multiple wings thrust upward as if to signify great power. Behind the angel was an assemblage of babies in paradise in different positions of honor, awe and respect. At the angel's feet was the same curly red headed ruddy cheeked Baby in Paradise I had seen previously. The Baby in Paradise held on to the front of the garment or robe that was ankle length to show respect and was turned upward in a look of awe to the angel's face. The angel did not say anything to me.

The reason for these visions only became clear to me in March in the year of 1986. God was again asking me, "Have I taken care of the babies in paradise?"

CHAPTER THIRTY FOUR

VISION OF MARY, MOTHER OF GOD AND THE HALO ON THE MOON

December, 1986

I wrote this on December 13, 2011. More complete details of this vision were mailed a few nights after the vision to Mary Fugate, Dayton, Ohio. She was a good friend and was single at that time. She never returned to me the original copy I wrote of this vision while it was really fresh in my mind. She kept it for a souvenir. I have recreated it here as well as I can. This vision occurred in a dark winter evening at my home at Deer Cliff Run south of Tipp City, Ohio at the end of my driveway.

I was in the kitchen and I thought I heard many voices out in the garage. There is a doorway from the kitchen to the garage. It is a two car garage and has two separate garage doors. I thought maybe friends came over or neighbors were in the driveway in front of the garage. I opened the door from the kitchen to the garage, but I did not turn on the lights. As I opened both overhead doors to the garage with the battery operated remote opener, this brought on some automatic lighting. To my surprise, I did not see anyone standing there. Next, I went into the garage and then walked out into the driveway. I stood there and looked all around. There was no one to be seen. I walked forward to the end of the driveway not 10 feet from the asphalt street. The driveway is not very long and ends at a cudasak. At this time I heard those same voices behind me. The lights in the garage door opener are on a timer and they shut off so I was in the darkness of night.

The voices behind me continued. I did not turn around because then I suspected it was spirits. I did not desire to see this. They all shouted, "On your knees before your Lord's mother, Mary! Respect the woman that bore your Lord Jesus and taught him to be good to men." At that same time I could feel a hand into my back between my shoulder blades and it pushed me forward a little then I felt more hands on the top of my shoulders pressing me down to my knees. I almost lost my wind as it was such a forceful push.

The voices argued and I could not understand all that they were saying. Then a different voice said, "He should lie on his stomach prostration with his hands reaching out to his Lord's mother. He should be praying for her blessings. He must learn the meaning of respect for our lady Mary, the mother of God, so he may tell others." I retorted back to them while I was still facing away from them towards the street, "I will pray on my knees to the most Holy Mary, Mother of God. I cannot lay prostration (on my stomach) as my back hurts. I promise to listen to your instructions and that of our Lord's mother, Mary."

The voices discussed this some more with words that I could not understand what they said because they whispered. I thought that I dare not to look behind at them or they might force me to the ground on my stomach. One of them said, "You may stay on your knees because you need to see and listen to what Mary wants from you." Then I could see Mary up in the evening sky, emanating a glow of light as she had a light from within. For this reason, it was easy to see her body features and the expression of compassion in her face. She was about fifty feet away from me standing in the sky about twenty feet above the ground. She did not stand on anything that I could see. I heard voices of the angels from above Mary singing to me, but I did not see the angels this time.

She had the appearance of a woman in her late 40's. She wore a cloth scarf over her head but it did not hide any of her face. The scarf was light blue and she wore a robe of light gray or off white. She had a small mouth and thin lips. Her eyes were warm, but I could not determine her eye color because the lighting was dim. She had high cheek bones with a light brown complexion. I could just barely make out that she had either black hair or dark brown hair. Her chin was small but graceful in appearance. She looked much like the paintings and sculptures I have seen of her in churches and museums.

The angels were singing,

> "Hallelujah! Hallelujah! Hallelujah!
> Praise to our Holy of Holies Mary, mother of Christ.
> She is the most holy woman that ever lived. Praise to her!
> Hallelujah! Hallelujah! Hallelujah!
> May all the men and women of the world sing praise to our
> Mary!
> Hallelujah! Hallelujah! Hallelujah!
> She is most wonderful and filled with love and God's grace.
> She is the purest woman that there ever was.
> We love our mother of our Lord, Jesus.
> Hallelujah! Hallelujah! Hallelujah!
>
> She has come to the world to this man to teach him.
> She wants him to understand that women have a special place
> in heaven.
> And so they should have a special place in the world as
> well.
> They have the burden to bring into the world new souls.
> Hallelujah! Hallelujah! Hallelujah!
>
> Praise be to this man that he may understand that all men
> should respect women.
> They should hold them with reverence and grace.

Men should carry some of their burden to lessen their burden
in life.
Hallelujah! Hallelujah! Hallelujah!"

Then the voices that were behind me sang out,

"Look above sir to the heavenly hosts that escort our Lady
Mary.
They sing much praise for she is here to remind men that
women need respect.
Praise to the man who respects women for God shall reward
them for their deeds
Hallelujah! Hallelujah! Hallelujah!"

Then all the angels above Mary and the heavenly persons who are
behind me all sang out,

"Hallelujah! Hallelujah! Hallelujah!
Bring the lessons to our prophet. Tell him to tell others.
Hallelujah! Hallelujah! Hallelujah!
Our kingdom is good and holy. Our kingdom is with God.
Mary is most holy. She is the most High.
Our Lord's mother is mother of the world.
She must be held in high esteem.
Hallelujah! Hallelujah! Hallelujah!"

Then the heavenly persons or angels behind me put their hands on
my shoulders and on my stomach. Mary said,

"Let his life force go to the heavens. Let him be
reminded forever to know what respect and caring
concern for Mary mother of our Lord means. Let him
teach others of this respect for women.

Hallelujah! Hallelujah! Hallelujah!"

Then I saw a beam of lighted energy about 12 inches in diameter emit from my stomach and reach all the way to the full moon. It appeared to me that the light struck the moon and then shot outward from the moon such that it resembled wagon wheel spokes. This caused a large brilliant halo that was about the moon. I was awe struck for it was most impressive. I stared at the halo for what seemed like 10 minutes. It stayed there most of the night. Friends told me the beam of light and halo about the moon was seen by other persons living miles away from my house. I never saw any angels but I saw Mary, mother of Jesus in the heavens as she looked over me with great care and concern. She is a beautiful and holy person.

I learned a valuable lesson that evening. A man should never forget his respect for a good woman and he should take care to lessen her burden in life whenever possible. If a man should stray from this lesson then he should plead for forgiveness from his spiritual mother Mary. She is the spiritual mother of all persons in this world. Lord, please forgive them for their sins and any time they do not remember this valuable lesson. Amen

Women are people like men and they carry sins. Some women are very bad and evil. It is important though that man be able to discriminate between the good women and the bad women. Men should respect the good women but not be tricked or forced into losing their faith over a bad woman.

CHAPTER THIRTY FIVE

THE MIRACLE WHEN I SURVIVED A LIFE THREATENING ILLNESS

Spring, 1995

I wrote this on January 19, 2012. Originally I did not plan to include these events in this book because it did not contain any reference to visions or angels. My friends heard this story from me several times and said it should be included because it was a miracle from God.

This incident began when I was scheduled to travel in the spring of 1995 to the United Kingdom for a design review of a proposed new oxygen generating system for Navy and Air Force military fighter aircraft. One of the companies doing this work was a British manufacturing company based in Yeovil, Somerset, England. They manufactured high altitude life support equipment for the aerospace industry. The day before this trip at work I noticed a pain in my lower abdomen. It felt something like someone had punched me very hard in my lower abdomen with their fist. A coworker said it might be appendicitis as he had experienced that before. I had been having lots of muscle spasm problems from injuries received during a previous automobile accident years ago. I thought with some stretching exercises this problem and resulting pain would go away.

The next day I boarded the flight to United Kingdom and was on my way to one of the worst experiences I had ever had in my life. I arrived at a London airport without any problems early in the morning but I was not feeling too well. I felt weak and ill. I was with a team of Navy persons while I was representing the Air Force. We drove south from London to Yeovil, Somerset, England. It took most of that day. By the time we had arrived I was really feeling ill. I just thought that I needed some rest. I turned in for sleep early that evening.

I awoke sooner than I needed to get up which was very early in the morning just at sunrise. I sat up on the edge of bed. I noticed a very bad pain in my lower abdomen and I felt feverish and tired. Having traveled so far to be at this meeting, I was trapped, so to speak, since all there was to do would be to go to the meeting. I went to the meeting but after a few hours I noticed I was not able to sit upright without severe pain in my lower abdomen. I attended the rest of the meeting by lying down on some chairs in the back of the room. I could still hear the briefing for the design review. By the mid-afternoon I felt it wise to go see a doctor.

One of the military team members drove me to a local doctor where I had to sit and wait in excess of an hour. After that amount of time I was almost in an emergency situation being in really severe pain. I had some pain pills with me because I had suffered neck and back injuries several years ago in an auto accident. My family doctor in Beavercreek, Ohio made sure I always had this medicine in case I needed it. I did need the medicine to get to sleep most nights. This was all that kept me going. The doctor finally did see me, but he only took blood and urine samples. Later he said I had diabetes. I don't think he was much of a doctor because diabetes would not cause the extreme pain I was experiencing. So we left. The next day a kind lady in the English company drove me to another doctor in a nearby larger town. They only argued over how I was to pay for the medical service. My government health insurance would cover this, but they did not trust this. I see socialized medicine doctors can't even recognize an emergency medical issue to respond quickly. Eventually, the kind lady who drove me to this clinic was able to get them to see me. This doctor only gave me a quick examination without any testing whatsoever. He stated I must have a muscle strain or a torn ligament. In the United Kingdom they have socialized medicine. So I learned about the issues in dealing with the medical profession in a country with socialized medicine. Their health care did not appear to be very good. He did give me a prescription of pain medicine. The medicine made me see different colored stars exploding in my eye sight.

The meeting came to an end and there was a party that evening at a local pub. I went to this because I was nauseous and was not able to eat anything for the whole day. I did manage to get down some lager ale and eat some English beef stew. The next day we drove back to London to go back to the United States as the meeting was over. The team stopped at several locations for sight seeing. One place I clearly remember was a run down castle. I remember there was a band of gypsies at one of the fields near the castle. They had large horses and a colorful wagon like you see on the television shows but you rarely see in the real world. I could only lie down in the back of the automobile and wait on the others government team members to come back.

Finally, the team made it to London where we stayed overnight at a hotel near the airport. We planned to fly out the next morning. I stayed in my room because I was really feeling very ill and feverish by this time. I tried taking a hot bath, but it did not help. I then realized I was seriously ill and maybe even dying. I remember at that time I was very scared and got down on my knees facing the bedside. I prayed to God to remember me and be it his will please let me live. I love this life here and I did not want to leave so soon. Someone on the hotel staff knocked on my door and asked if I was alright. I said yes. Later after he left I thought that was a mistake. I did need help. I was approached in the morning by some of the team members who wanted to take me to a hospital in the London area. I did not trust the doctors in this country from my past experience with the last two doctors so I declined to be taken to the hospital. I was thinking if I could just make it back to Dayton, Ohio I would be saved. I wanted to go the emergency room of the Grand View Hospital. That could have been a big mistake as I could have died on the flight back home. Fortunately I did not die.

We went to the airport and the only way I was able to make it back to the gate was to be driven by an electric vehicle inside the terminal. One of the Navy team members helped me. I was barely able to walk. The flight back to the United States took many hours. The flight crew found out about my sickness and offered to land in New York City to take me to a hospital. All I could think about was to get home to Dayton and go to Grand View Hospital. I knew that they had very good emergency service. I knew this because I had been taken there previously, thinking I had a heart attack. I was most impressed with their emergency care they performed to save my life. So I told the flight crew I'd be alright to go on to Dayton. In retrospect I think I made a bad decision but I was not thinking very clearly at that time. Here again, I could have died trying to get to the hospital in Dayton. The flight attendants even offered to call an ambulance to drive me to the hospital and I declined again. I should have let them call an ambulance. After arriving at Dayton airport parking, I went to pick up my automobile. The parking attendant told me I really looked very ill as my face was white as a ghost.

When I drove to the emergency room at Grand View Hospital, I could hardly keep the car on the road. I remember walking into the emergency care area at the hospital which was a 15 minute drive from the airport and telling the doctor I was dying. He laughed and said; "Only people that come to our emergency room in a stretcher are dying. You are walking in." I had brought in all my prescription medicine so they would know what I had been taking. They immediately run a CAT scan test. The doctor came back and said my intestine was torn open and the contents of my large colon were into my abdominal cavity. He showed me the negative X-ray of my lower abdomen which showed a great amount of bowel in my abdomen. The X-ray showed it was all over my abdominal cavity because that part of the negative was clear. On the X-ray that means there is something there that is solid. In this case, it was my bowel. He said, "You are dying! We need to get you to surgery right away!" They rushed me into an operating room and technician or nurse pushed a plastic hose quickly up my nose to my stomach. They started pumping out the contents of my stomach and it was a greenish fluid. The nurse said, "See we are helping you already. Look at the poison coming out of your stomach."

They put me under with an anesthetic. I have no further recollection of anything for several days. I will relate the time periods that I do remember, but I cannot be sure of the order of events. I was very ill at that time and on the verge of dying.

The next thing I remember was that I was unable to sufficiently breathe. I could breathe but I could not get enough air to sustain me. I was just semi-conscious and barely knew what was going on or where I was. I desperately used my tongue to loosen whatever was fastened to my mouth and lips. It was some type of tape. Finally, I got the tape loose and I worked this tube out of my mouth with my tongue and I spit it out. Then I heard loud dinging sounds and ladies making frantic voices about something. They were thinking I was dying. Since they thought I was not breathing, they frantically came to my bedside. There was a tube from a ventilator in my mouth and I had spit it out. I came to full consciousness then and I heard the doctor say that, "If he can breathe on his own, clearly he does not need the ventilator." My wife was talking to the doctor asking him how I was and I heard the doctor reply, "It seems he is better if he can breathe on his own." I just needed more volume of oxygen than the ventilator was giving to me. I have large lungs.

Much later, a male nurse came in and talked to me. We were alone. He was telling me they did several surgeries on me and it was days later from when I first came into the hospital. He showed me that my abdomen was still open and had a quick-release string holding it together. He said my lower abdomen was being cleaned by a machine like people's blood is sometimes cleaned by dialysis. The male nurse increased my medicine dose and this made me lose consciousness again. In the doctor's terminology I was in a medically induced coma.

The next thing I remember was being awakened in intensive care. The surgeons and my wife were standing what to me looked like 50 feet away from my bed. Later, my wife said they were all standing much closer. My surgeon asked me to sit up in bed. There were all sorts of wires and tubes connected to me. I felt like a marionette puppet. The doctor asked me to stand up and walk towards him. It was difficult to sit up. A nurse helped me to sit up. I then carefully slid off the side of the gurney and stood up. I had all sorts of wires and tubes connected to my body trailing behind me. I felt so weak and depressed. I remember saying to the surgeon, "Why don't you just let me die in peace?" The surgeon then said something about giving me more blood plasma. I lay down and the nurse spoke kind words to me asking me to hang in there. Next thing I knew I'm out again in a medically induced coma.

At one point in the coma I remember distinctly that I was trying to awaken. It was like I was a tiny person inside my head and he was trying to crawl out of my eye socket or my mouth but I was not able to make it. Also at times, I felt like I was in a one dimensional room crawling around on the floor and not able to get up or get into bed. It was a very restricted feeling. Sometimes I was on the bed trapped there and not able to move from it.

One time I had this dream that I was suddenly in an old hospital room with lime green walls which were painted with lighter and darker lime green colors. I was facing an office with windows that were frosted. It had Venetian blinds and a door on the right side of the window. I could not see into that room. There was a hallway on my left side that went somewhere. I could not tell where it went though as it was so long it faded into the distance. This room was like a hospital room in the 1940's. I remembered thinking I was in St. Louis, Missouri but I do not know why. There were perhaps 15 persons standing in the same room I was in who were in front of this office. They were all looking straight at me. There were priests, rabbis, pastors, nuns and other religious persons. They all said, "Now is not your time!" About five of the persons including a nun and another woman who looked like a nurse took hold of my arms. They laid me forcibly back onto a gurney which had maroon red leather like covering. They said, "We will fix your illness and send you back." I could see over my lower eye lids they had their hands in my lower abdomen rearranging my insides. The next thing I knew I am back in the hospital at Grand View with surgeons and nurses all around me. The surgeon said, "We thought we lost you. You flat lined." He asked me if I had an experience like seeing light or deceased relatives coming to get me. I said no, but I explained that I was in the hospital room with religious leaders who said now is not my time. They said they would fix me and send me back. He said that was it. I was just in some part of heaven. Many persons who nearly die experience something like this.

Once in the evening I recalled one of the intensive care nurses woke me. She spoke kind sweet words to me and asked me to awaken. I woke up and she asked me to sit up. She looked at me very sternly and said, "Mister, you are not going to die on my watch. You're going to fight to live. I'm going to get you to eat some food." I had been on a feeding tube for over a week. She left and when she was gone she got candy, potato chips, pop cycles and ice cream all out of vending machines and then came back to me. She asked me to eat what I could. All I could eat was a little ice cream out of a small cardboard tub. I remember the small wooden spoon. It would not go into the frozen ice cream so well. After she saw I could not eat anymore, she helped me to lie down again because I was very tired. I slowly passed out again.

Another time I remember having a dream that I was in a display window and I was sitting in a barber's chair that was moving up and down and around. People were walking by and watching me. Then I awoke and found I was on a special chair in a different part of the hospital with a pulsating suit over my legs. It made me want to urinate so I yelled at the attendants who were in another room talking and laughing. They unhooked me and I went to the bathroom. I finished the session with the pulsating suit and they took me back to my bed. At the hospital bed the nurse again put me under in a medically induced coma. Later, it was explained to me that this device is used to stimulate blood circulation in the legs to prevent bed sores or blood clots.

Sometime later I was awakened and both of my surgeons were standing there. They explained the whole series of surgeries and procedures I had been through the past week or so. They explained I had a cyst on my large colon called diverticulitis. Diverticulitis is swelling or inflammation of an abnormal wall or is pouches in the intestinal wall. These pouches are usually found in the large colon. Mine was at the turning location of the large colon as it goes to the last one third of the large colon. They said it was on the outside of the wall of my colon, on the back side and there was a lot of infection within a large cyst. They had performed one surgery removing the last part of my large colon because it was perforated with infection. I did not get well so the team of doctors decided to put a dye into my stomach and they found that there was still a leak through a small hole on my large colon. It was on the backside at the bend where it goes down to the last one third of my large colon. The doctors said it was covered by a maze of blood vessels so they missed it the first surgery. That is why it was so hard to locate. It had ruptured causing my condition. They told me many doctors and nurses had worked extra hard trying to save my life. They then did a second surgery and removed another one third of my large colon. It was the part that goes across the abdomen. They also removed my appendix so no doctor would never again have to go in and operate on the first one third of my large colon. They showed me I had a colostomy at my right side high up on my abdomen to be out of the healing area of the inside of my abdomen. There were holes at the lower part of my abdomen with tubes in them to drain what they called slough. They said I was not out of the woods yet and that I could still die.

The surgeons explained to me later that it was God's miracle that I survived. No one in medical history had survived past 3 days with a ruptured colon. The bowel with its deadly bacteria infection usually goes straight to the heart and kidneys. They said I must have had a very strong guardian angel looking out for me. I had survived in excess of 7 days with an open colon even before I got to the hospital. They told me I taught the surgeons that it was possible to save someone with an open colon past 3 days and they would have to rewrite the medical books. Much later, the doctors and nurses said I must have something important to finish in this world before I am taken by death. Well, for years I thought it was that God wanted to show that lives could be saved past 3 days with an open colon. But later in my life I now believe it is that I must complete this book and get all this information to the public. This information is after all much of God's, the angels and the heavenly person's words. While I was still recovering in the hospital, doctors and nurses were all stopping by to see me. When doctors and nurses are on tours in the hospital they have a list of patients to visit. A doctor would say to them, "You will not see this in another 100 years. This patient survived a ruptured colon past 3 days. It was a miracle." Many doctors and nurses came by to see my abdomen and look at my X-rays.

I had another serious problem with my back as it hurt very much. They gave me physical therapy every day but it did not seem to help much. I remember walking as much as possible around the hallways on my floor where my bed was located. Bandages would fall all over the floor. The nurses would laugh and giggle and follow me sometimes and pick up the bandages. They were always putting clean bandages over my wounds on my abdomen. The nurses encouraged me to walk as much as possible. The nurses had to change the dressings over my wounds about every four hours if I recall correctly. They handled me like I had a contagious disease. So the scissors would be put in special disposal containers along with my used bandages and dressings.

After being released from the hospital after nearly three weeks, I had to constantly walk to keep healing. If I did not walk I would begin to feel ill. I remember sitting on the couch watching this television show about people being frozen in liquid nitrogen after death. I felt like I was dead and my body was cold throughout. The walking overcame this cold feeling. It was terrifying because I was worried every day I would die. About 6 months later I had reconstructive surgery to reconnect my large colon so there would be no more colostomy. It was a very cold winter day with lots of snow on the ground. The doctors ask my permission to take television video of the surgery so this could be used for training other doctors. I gave the permission.

Later, I developed a hernia where the colostomy had been and I needed major surgery again on my abdomen. I had to have a fabric patch to cover the rupture in my abdomen lining to keep my organs inside.

This whole ordeal was the most astounding experience I had ever been through. I remember they gave me counseling because they thought I would be self-conscious with the colostomy and bag on my upper abdomen. I was not self conscious at all. I told everyone I was just happy to still be alive.

Ten years later my back became very bad and I was in extreme pain. It turned out that I had degenerative disc disease and it took 3 surgeons 5 hours to repair my lower spine and discs. Since then, I have not had pains in my back except the muscles when they are over stressed. I thank God and his angels for saving my life and allowing me to live many more years so I could complete this book. Recently I had to have more surgery to correct my right shoulder. I had a torn rotator cup, arthritis in the joint, missing cartridge at the end of the small bone that comes from the neck. Apparently, this had been missing because of a genetic defect. It took me 6 months of physical therapy to get back some fraction of my shoulder strength. I now am in physical therapy again to build up my strength of my back, stomach and shoulder because six major surgeries has left me much weaker.

CHAPTER THIRTY SIX

VISION AT THE FUNERAL OF MY STEP-FATHER, LEWIS EDWARD KIMBERLING

February 22, 1997

This was written on December 13, 2011. In the few months before my step-father's death, I had long conversations with Lewis about his fears of dying. We sat on our screened in porch at Jamesport, Missouri. He had colon cancer that had been with him for about 16 years. It had spread to his spine where it was now inoperable. He knew he would die soon in the coming months so he was greatly concerned about what would be there for him after that. He lived and hung tightly on to life as long as he could because he wanted to take care of his wife and my mother, Mary Ann. He knew I've seen angels most of my life so he wanted to talk to me about life after death. He said he was having disturbing nightmares about dropping into a dark abyss with no bottom in sight and he would be lost. He told me he had this great fear about dying and was having these terrible nightmares. This greatly troubled him and he wanted to know what I could tell him about life after death. I told him the angels tell me there is heaven and hell and if he accepts God into his life he will live forever in heaven. His faith must be strong. I also told him that things

218

would be different for him as he would be a spirit and not a material person. Also, he most likely would not be able to contact those still in the world. He said that was alright as he just wanted to know that there was something after death. I said I was pretty certain of this based on my numerous visions with angels. Also angels had taken my spirit body to heaven and the edge of hell. This greatly pleased him and he was more at ease.

When I left to go back to work in Dayton, Ohio it was just after Christmas. I did not realize it that death was so close for Lewis. He got worse very quickly. The entire family was in the room where he was drawing his last breaths. The family called me so I could speak some words over the telephone on his passing. You know it really challenged my faith to see someone I knew and loved so long pass on. I hope to keep my faith when I face death as this is the glue that holds me to God. When I think about his fears it sometimes sends shudders down my back because I know someday I will also die. Everyone will die sometime.

I quickly returned to Jamesport, Missouri for the visitation and the funeral. The reverend of the Jamesport United Methodist Church asked me to say the eulogy. When I got up in front to speak to the persons at the church about Lewis, I gulped a lot and had trouble getting the words out. I had written the following eulogy which is given below. Toward the end of my eulogy I heard my step-father say, "You were right Dennis. There is a life after death." I looked up to see an entire host of angels under a rainbow. They were in the clouds. They were singing salutations to God. Then I also saw two angels carrying my step-father Lewis upward to the clouds. There was an angel on each side holding onto his upper arms. When I saw that, the words got stuck in my mouth briefly. My knees felt weak and I nearly lost my balance and fell away from the pedestal. All in my family liked my prose for his eulogy. I told my mother about the angels carrying her husband to heaven because I thought it would give her some peace.

Lewis Edward Kimberling Eulogy

When I first heard Lewis had passed away
I remembered the things he did that made him happy,
   his woodworking projects and inventions.
His family was his life.
Dad struggled a long 16 years with his illness, cancer.
He had many surgeries and stays at the hospital.
He had to deal with a lot of pain.
My mother, Mary Ann, took good care of him though.
Lewis cared a lot about his family and he always tried
   to take care of his children and grandchildren.
He was a very good man, a husband, father, brother and
   grandfather.
I know he loved all his family and children very much.
I know also he loved my mother, Mary Ann, very much.
They were married 45 years.
Last year we spoke on the porch.
Lewis was worried if I was alright after my illness two years
   ago.
He was also concerned if I still had my faith.
That was Lewis, a caring father. I think he left something
   wonderful for all of us to remember him by.
I think that is the truest expression of love!
Dad I know you are with your family in heaven now.
You are with God now.
All the family you left behind will truly miss you.
I know I will miss you very much.

Peace be with you.
Dennis

Lewis Edward Kimberling
Birth December 17, 1912
Death February 22, 1997

Jamesport, Missouri

Age 84 years and 2 months

I did not know it then, but this would be the last time I would see any angels or have any significant visions. I do, however, still have that help from God and his angels when I pray. Sometimes I am given glimpses of what God plans for the future of man. I have used this to make sure this book is accurate as I can possibly make it.

CHAPTER THIRTY SEVEN

PROPHETS IN THIS MODERN AGE

I realize there are many persons living in this modern world that believe all this Christianity with angels and prophets occurred in the past thousands of years ago and it is no longer with us. Many think that God, if he does exist at all, has forgotten us. Attendance at many churches is falling rapidly in recent times. Many people have been forgetting God and they think he is just a fairy tale from the distant past. The faith of many, if it still exists, is lessening.

I have strong faith in our Lord. I have been a witness to God's wonders and he has spoken to me face to face. I want to tell you that God is still here with us now more than ever. My visions have left no doubt in my mind about God and his many legions of angels. There are still miracles everywhere in the world. The world news seems to only report bad news and not the good news. People may be reluctant to believe it is even possible there is a prophet in these times. Many will think it is madness.

I think people now should realize that God and his angels are everywhere with compassion and love for all men and women. Also, Satan is here as well to help us forget God. The Bible speaks to this issue and I want to provide all some advice in the Bible that still applies today about prophets and angels. <u>Remember this above all</u>

else, it is a sin to despise any prophesying should it favor God. Instead despise Satan and his evil doings so that you will give away your sins. This is true no matter the form Satan or his demons may take. Pray to God for insight into differentiating the difference.

What the Bible has to say about prophesying and how shall you treat the stranger you find who prophesizes is stated below.

1 Thessalonians 5:12-28 (Original King James Version)

Final Instructions

"[12]And we beseech you, brethren, to know them which labour among you, and are over you in the Lord, and admonish you;

[13]And to esteem them very highly in love for their work's sake. And be at peace among yourselves.

[14]Now we exhort you, brethren, warn them that are unruly, comfort the feebleminded, support the weak, be patient toward all men.

[15]See that none render evil for evil unto any man; but ever follow that which is good, both among yourselves, and to all men.

[16]Rejoice evermore.

[17]Pray without ceasing.

[18]In every thing give thanks: for this is the will of God in Christ Jesus concerning you.

[19]Quench not the Spirit.

[20]Despise not prophesyings.

[21]Prove all things; hold fast that which is good.

[22]Abstain from all appearance of evil.

23And the very God of peace sanctify you wholly; and I pray God your whole spirit and soul and body be preserved blameless unto the coming of our Lord Jesus Christ.

24Faithful is he that calleth you, who also will do it.

25Brethren, pray for us.

26Greet all the brethren with a holy kiss.

27I charge you by the Lord that this epistle be read unto all the holy brethren.

28The grace of our Lord Jesus Christ be with you. Amen."

Prophesizing by People is Discussed in the Scriptures

I want to tell you about what the Scriptures say about people prophesizing. Should the people whether in church or not judge me with malice in their hearts. This is considered a sin against the workings of God. My prophesizing is discussed in the Scriptures. This is given below for all readers to know the past words of wisdom.

2 Thessalonians 1:1-12 (Original King James Version)

"1Paul, and Silvanus, and Timotheus, unto the church of the Thessalonians in God our Father and the Lord Jesus Christ:

2Grace unto you, and peace, from God our Father and the Lord Jesus Christ.

3We are bound to thank God always for you, brethren, as it is meet, because that your faith groweth exceedingly, and the charity of every one of you all toward each other aboundeth;

4So that we ourselves glory in you in the churches of God for your patience and faith in all your persecutions and tribulations that ye endure:

⁵Which is a manifest token of the righteous judgment of God, that ye may be counted worthy of the kingdom of God, for which ye also suffer:

⁶Seeing it is a righteous thing with God to recompense tribulation to them that trouble you;

⁷And to you who are troubled rest with us, when the Lord Jesus shall be revealed from heaven with his mighty angels,

⁸In flaming fire taking vengeance on them that know not God, and that obey not the gospel of our Lord Jesus Christ:

⁹Who shall be punished with everlasting destruction from the presence of the Lord, and from the glory of his power;

¹⁰When he shall come to be glorified in his saints, and to be admired in all them that believe (because our testimony among you was believed) in that day.

¹¹Wherefore also we pray always for you, that our God would count you worthy of this calling, and fulfill all the good pleasure of his goodness, and the work of faith with power:

¹²That the name of our Lord Jesus Christ may be glorified in you, and ye in him, according to the grace of our God and the Lord Jesus Christ."

CHAPTER THIRTY EIGHT

TROUBLE MAKERS ABUSING CHRISTIANS AND PROPHETS

The Bible has advice concerning trouble makers and idle people who disrupt the word of the Lord. Regarding the spreading of the new word of God, trouble makers and idle people should beware, according to that advice already given below in the Scriptures.

2 Thessalonians 3:1-10 (Original King James Version)

Request for Prayer

"¹Finally, brethren, pray for us, that the word of the Lord may have free course, and be glorified, even as it is with you:

²And that we may be delivered from unreasonable and wicked men: for all men have not faith.

³But the Lord is faithful, who shall stablish you, and keep you from evil.

⁴And we have confidence in the Lord touching you, that ye both do and will do the things which we command you.

⁵And the Lord direct your hearts into the love of God, and into the patient waiting for Christ.

⁶Now we command you, brethren, in the name of our Lord Jesus Christ, that ye withdraw yourselves from every brother that walketh disorderly, and not after the tradition which he received of us.

⁷For yourselves know how ye ought to follow us: for we behaved not ourselves disorderly among you;

⁸Neither did we eat any man's bread for nought; but wrought with labour and travail night and day, that we might not be chargeable to any of you:

⁹Not because we have not power, but to make ourselves an ensample unto you to follow us.

¹⁰For even when we were with you, this we commanded you, that if any would not work, neither should he eat.

CHAPTER THIRTY NINE

THE COMING OF THE LORD AND JUDGMENT TIME

God has asked me to tell you what the Bible has to say about the coming of the Lord and Judgment time. This has been prophesized now for many years. The Holy Spirit came to the world at Pentecost and this is still with us today. Pentecost commemorates the descent of the Holy Spirit upon the Twelve Apostles and other followers of Jesus as described in the Acts of the Apostles 2:1–30. Pentecost among Christians is sometimes described as the "Birthday of the Church." The Bible describes Pentecost when the 12 Disciples of Christ (Acts 1:13-26) among over hundred and twenty other individuals (Acts 1:15), received the Baptism in the Holy Spirit in the upper room. This is given in the second chapter of the Book of Acts. As recounted in Acts 2:1–6. Many women, including Mary the mother of Jesus, (Acts 1:14) also received the Holy Spirit.

And the angel of the Lord did tell me to include this entire chapter of Acts 2:1-30. I also want to explain that many persons do not know this ended the Age of the Law with Moses and started the age of compassion and love with Jesus as our Savior. The Holy Spirit that was let loose this day is still with us today waiting on people to accept our Lord as their Savior and be filled with the Spirit.

Acts 2:1-30 (Original King James Version which is in the public domain)

The Holy Spirit Comes at Pentecost

"¹And when the day of Pentecost was fully come, they were all with one accord in one place.

²And suddenly there came a sound from heaven as of a rushing mighty wind, and it filled all the house where they were sitting.

³And there appeared unto them cloven tongues like as of fire, and it sat upon each of them.

⁴And they were all filled with the Holy Ghost, and began to speak with other tongues, as the Spirit gave them utterance.

⁵And there were dwelling at Jerusalem Jews, devout men, out of every nation under heaven.

⁶Now when this was noised abroad, the multitude came together, and were confounded, because that every man heard them speak in his own language.

⁷And they were all amazed and marvelled, saying one to another, Behold, are not all these which speak Galilaeans?

⁸And how hear we every man in our own tongue, wherein we were born?

⁹Parthians, and Medes, and Elamites, and the dwellers in Mesopotamia, and in Judaea, and Cappadocia, in Pontus, and Asia,

¹⁰Phrygia, and Pamphylia, in Egypt, and in the parts of Libya about Cyrene, and strangers of Rome, Jews and proselytes,

¹¹Cretes and Arabians, we do hear them speak in our tongues the wonderful works of God.

[12]And they were all amazed, and were in doubt, saying one to another, What meaneth this?

[13]Others mocking said, These men are full of new wine.

[14]But Peter, standing up with the eleven, lifted up his voice, and said unto them, Ye men of Judaea, and all ye that dwell at Jerusalem, be this known unto you, and hearken to my words:

[15]For these are not drunken, as ye suppose, seeing it is but the third hour of the day.

[16]But this is that which was spoken by the prophet Joel;

[17]And it shall come to pass in the last days, saith God, I will pour out of my Spirit upon all flesh: and your sons and your daughters shall prophesy, and your young men shall see visions, and your old men shall dream dreams:

[18]And on my servants and on my handmaidens I will pour out in those days of my Spirit; and they shall prophesy:

[19]And I will shew wonders in heaven above, and signs in the earth beneath; blood, and fire, and vapour of smoke:

[20]The sun shall be turned into darkness, and the moon into blood, before the great and notable day of the Lord come:

[21]And it shall come to pass, that whosoever shall call on the name of the Lord shall be saved.

[22]Ye men of Israel, hear these words; Jesus of Nazareth, a man approved of God among you by miracles and wonders and signs, which God did by him in the midst of you, as ye yourselves also know:

[23]Him, being delivered by the determinate counsel and foreknowledge of God, ye have taken, and by wicked hands have crucified and slain:

²⁴Whom God hath raised up, having loosed the pains of death: because it was not possible that he should be holden of it.

²⁵For David speaketh concerning him, I foresaw the Lord always before my face, for he is on my right hand, that I should not be moved:

²⁶Therefore did my heart rejoice, and my tongue was glad; moreover also my flesh shall rest in hope:

²⁷Because thou wilt not leave my soul in hell, neither wilt thou suffer thine Holy One to see corruption.

²⁸Thou hast made known to me the ways of life; thou shalt make me full of joy with thy countenance.

²⁹Men and brethren, let me freely speak unto you of the patriarch David, that he is both dead and buried, and his sepulchre is with us unto this day.

³⁰Therefore being a prophet, and knowing that God had sworn with an oath to him, that of the fruit of his loins, according to the flesh, he would raise up Christ to sit on his throne;

CHAPTER FORTY

SIGNS OF THE COMING OF CHRIST AND JUDGMENT TIME

The Lord had asked me to tell everyone about the coming of Christ and judgment time. In the last age and at the time before Christ returns, what everyone should know is that there will be an awakening of prophesizing because, after the messenger has spoken, seven more prophets will come and say many wondrous things. This is the beginning of the Third Age. People should be aware that the time is getting short. No longer should people put off making peace with God. It is time many should turn away from evil ways and turn to Christ, God and the Holy Spirit to be saved. God had asked me to tell all that the time of the modern prophets is beginning. God has chosen the author of this book to be the *messenger* announcing the new age and reform that God says is needed. The time for those ancient prophesies that have been spoken and recorded in the Bible, which have not already been fulfilled, will come to pass soon. All should look for more prophets in this final age of the world where the Holy Spirit of the Lord will rain down upon the world much as rain comes in a heavy thunderstorm. The prophets will shake the foundation of the world just as the thunder and lightning shakes the souls of men. Be not afraid, but embrace the wonders of the new words and the prophesizing. God wants many to turn away from sinning, seek forgiveness and ask for the saving grace.

Joel 2:1-32 (Original King James Version)

An Army of Locusts

"¹Blow ye the trumpet in Zion, and sound an alarm in my holy mountain: let all the inhabitants of the land tremble: for the day of the LORD cometh, for it is nigh at hand;

²A day of darkness and of gloominess, a day of clouds and of thick darkness, as the morning spread upon the mountains: a great people and a strong; there hath not been ever the like, neither shall be any more after it, even to the years of many generations.

³A fire devoureth before them; and behind them a flame burneth: the land is as the garden of Eden before them, and behind them a desolate wilderness; yea, and nothing shall escape them.

⁴The appearance of them is as the appearance of horses; and as horsemen, so shall they run.

⁵Like the noise of chariots on the tops of mountains shall they leap, like the noise of a flame of fire that devoureth the stubble, as a strong people set in battle array.

⁶Before their face the people shall be much pained: all faces shall gather blackness.

⁷They shall run like mighty men; they shall climb the wall like men of war; and they shall march every one on his ways, and they shall not break their ranks:

⁸Neither shall one thrust another; they shall walk every one in his path: and when they fall upon the sword, they shall not be wounded.

⁹They shall run to and fro in the city; they shall run upon the wall, they shall climb up upon the houses; they shall enter in at the windows like a thief.

¹⁰The earth shall quake before them; the heavens shall tremble: the sun and the moon shall be dark, and the stars shall withdraw their shining:

¹¹And the LORD shall utter his voice before his army: for his camp is very great: for he is strong that executeth his word: for the day of the LORD is great and very terrible; and who can abide it?

¹²Therefore also now, saith the LORD, turn ye even to me with all your heart, and with fasting, and with weeping, and with mourning:

¹³And rend your heart, and not your garments, and turn unto the LORD your God: for he is gracious and merciful, slow to anger, and of great kindness, and repenteth him of the evil.

¹⁴Who knoweth if he will return and repent, and leave a blessing behind him; even a meat offering and a drink offering unto the LORD your God?

¹⁵Blow the trumpet in Zion, sanctify a fast, call a solemn assembly:

¹⁶Gather the people, sanctify the congregation, assemble the elders, gather the children, and those that suck the breasts: let the bridegroom go forth of his chamber, and the bride out of her closet.

¹⁷Let the priests, the ministers of the LORD, weep between the porch and the altar, and let them say, Spare thy people, O LORD, and give not thine heritage to reproach, that the heathen should rule over them: wherefore should they say among the people, Where is their God?

¹⁸Then will the LORD be jealous for his land, and pity his people.

¹⁹Yea, the LORD will answer and say unto his people, Behold, I will send you corn, and wine, and oil, and ye shall be satisfied therewith: and I will no more make you a reproach among the heathen:

²⁰But I will remove far off from you the northern army, and will drive him into a land barren and desolate, with his face toward the east sea, and his hinder part toward the utmost sea, and his stink shall come up, and his ill savour shall come up, because he hath done great things.

²¹Fear not, O land; be glad and rejoice: for the LORD will do great things.

²²Be not afraid, ye beasts of the field: for the pastures of the wilderness do spring, for the tree beareth her fruit, the fig tree and the vine do yield their strength.

²³Be glad then, ye children of Zion, and rejoice in the LORD your God: for he hath given you the former rain moderately, and he will cause to come down for you the rain, the former rain, and the latter rain in the first month.

²⁴And the floors shall be full of wheat, and the vats shall overflow with wine and oil.

²⁵And I will restore to you the years that the locust hath eaten, the cankerworm, and the caterpiller, and the palmerworm, my great army which I sent among you.

²⁶And ye shall eat in plenty, and be satisfied, and praise the name of the LORD your God, that hath dealt wondrously with you: and my people shall never be ashamed.

²⁷And ye shall know that I am in the midst of Israel, and that I am the LORD your God, and none else: and my people shall never be ashamed.

²⁸And it shall come to pass afterward, that I will pour out my spirit upon all flesh; and your sons and your daughters shall prophesy, your old men shall dream dreams, your young men shall see visions:

²⁹And also upon the servants and upon the handmaids in those days will I pour out my spirit.

³⁰And I will shew wonders in the heavens and in the earth, blood, and fire, and pillars of smoke.

³¹The sun shall be turned into darkness, and the moon into blood, before the great and terrible day of the LORD come.

³²And it shall come to pass, that whosoever shall call on the name of the LORD shall be delivered: for in mount Zion and in Jerusalem shall be deliverance, as the LORD hath said, and in the remnant whom the LORD shall call."

CHAPTER FORTY ONE

THE LESSON OF THE SERPENT FROM WHICH I BROKE FREE

God had reminded me that the lesson of the serpent and the dragon tells us of that which we should never forget. Only with God's assistance through a strong faith can we hope to defeat Satan on any day we might pass on and especially on that final day. Satan is an archangel and he is strong. When you ask for God's help, he gives you assistance to keep your faith in that time you face the dragon or the serpent. You can turn to the Bible to learn about the lesson of the serpent and the dragon. This is the same evil dragon that had me in its grasp at the edge of heaven and the beginning of hell. Remember these words on Judgment Day. Stand strong against the serpent or dragon and keep your armor of faith in God with you. When facing the dragon you will be afraid and this will shake your faith. So remember to ask God and his angels to save you, and then you surely will go to heaven. Do not let fear overtake your consciousness but keep the faith. If I teach anything to others it is this. Be strong and be with God.

Ephesians 6:10 through 6:20, "The Armor of God"

Last of all, I want to remind you that your strength must come from your faith in the Lord and this must come deep from within you. Put on all of God's armor so that you will be able to stand safe against all strategies and tricks of Satan. Satan will have many clever tricks to fool you. We are not fighting against people made of flesh and blood, but against persons without bodies. We are fighting against the evil rulers of the unseen world; those mighty satanic beings and great evil princes of darkness who rule the underworld; and against huge numbers of wicked spirits in this world. You will need the assistance of our Lord to have protection from these great evils.

So I remind you to use every piece of God's armor to resist the enemy whenever he attacks, and when it is all over, you will still be standing up and be strong of faith. But to do this, you will need the strong belt of truth and the breast plate of God's approval. Wear shoes that are able to speed you on as you preach the Good News of peace with God. In every battle you will need faith as your shield to stop the fiery arrows aimed at you by Satan and his evil demons. You will also need the helmet of salvation and the sword of the spirit which is the word of God.

Pray all the time. Ask God for anything in line with the Holy Spirit's wishes. Plead with him, reminding him of your needs and keep praying earnestly for yourself and all Christians everywhere.

1 Thessalonians 5:19-21

I want to remind you not to quench the spirit of your soul and Godliness. Also, do not sabotage the spirit of others about you but reinforce their faith and belief's in God.

2 Thessalonians 3:3

We should remember the Lord is always faithful and if you walk in the footsteps of a godly person he shall keep us strong and away from evil.

In all situations, try to prove valid all things which are good and holy. You should hold onto that which is good and holy.

Acts 2:16-21 and Joel 2:28-32

I should like to remind all concerning the prophesy of Joel regarding the coming of our Lord. It is time to pray for God's forgiveness of our sins, be saved and serve our Lord God.

God spoke through the prophet, Joel:

> *"And it shall come to pass in the last days, saith God, I will pour out my Spirit upon all flesh; and your sons and your daughters shall prophesy, and your young men shall see visions, and your old men shall dream dreams. And on my servants and on my handmaidens I will pour out in those days of my Spirit, and they shall prophesy. And I will show wonders in heaven above, and signs in the earth beneath: blood, and fire, and vapor of smoke. The sun shall be turned into darkness, and the moon into blood, before that great and notable day the Lord shall come; and it shall come to pass that whosoever shall call on the name of the Lord shall be saved."*

Those wonders that God is speaking about are part of the new age of mankind and the third great age with our Lord.

CHAPTER FORTY TWO

GOD SPEAKS TO ME OF MY RESPONSIBILITY

May 27, 1987

God did send to me another angel who told me about my role in all these visions and events that had occurred prior to this. The angel spoke to me concerning my responsibility. When God tells me words and gives me visions that are meant for many people then I must tell them. Ezekiel was told by God of the captivity of the people of the house of Israel about their future. Ezekiel knew they would hear these words but would not listen, so God told him he must tell them anyway to absolve himself of this responsibility. God had told him as given in Ezekiel 3:3-11. In Ezekiel 3:16-21 the prophet Ezekiel is told he must warn those who sin and do not turn away from their sinning that they will surely die in iniquity. As the watchman Ezekiel must tell others of the house of Israel that those who are righteous and continue to be righteous, they will live and have their souls delivered. God tells Ezekiel that as watchman it is his responsibility to tell those of the house of Israel about what God has warned them. As stated in Ezekiel 33:1-6, God says to Ezekiel that it is his responsibility for the sins of others if Ezekiel does not tell everyone of concern who will listen of his visions from God. Ezekiel is absolved of this burden when he freely tells all who will listen of his messages from God. God tells Isaiah similar warning in Isaiah 58:1.

Now I remember that God had told me, "As Ezekiel saw, you have seen. As he told the world so you must."

Ezekiel 33 (Original King James Version)

¹Again the word of the LORD came unto me, saying,

²Son of man, speak to the children of thy people, and say unto them, when I bring the sword upon a land, if the people of the land take a man of their coasts, and set him for their watchman:

³If when he seeth the sword come upon the land, he blow the trumpet, and warn the people;

⁴Then whosoever heareth the sound of the trumpet, and taketh not warning; if the sword come, and take him away, his blood shall be upon his own head.

⁵He heard the sound of the trumpet, and took not warning; his blood shall be upon him. But he that taketh warning shall deliver his soul.

⁶But if the watchman see the sword come, and blow not the trumpet, and the people be not warned; if the sword come, and take any person from among them, he is taken away in his iniquity; but his blood will I require at the watchman's hand.

For a long time I have thought that if I bend to the will of others too much and let them control me, then I am unhappy. I feel controlled and manipulated. My dignity is trampled. Then my thought is what will happen if I bend totally to the will of God. I will feel controlled by him perhaps and will I be unhappy? This is the trick that Satan so often uses to turn people away from God. He tried this with me. It is mentioned in this book in Chapter 17. In retrospect I think that I know God does not want this from me. I mean he does not want me to be unhappy. God wants me to exercise free will, follow righteousness, and be open to him but he will not totally take control of my will. So he does not ask this of you either. The self that is unique to each of us must coexist with God and his will. So I conclude that I must be mature and listen to thy Father, trust him and walk as a person happy with his self. Above all, I must love God, and then love myself next. I must love my family and neighbors as well. I think this is good words of advice for all others to follow as well.

I welcome those who seek my mission, to reach out and find sinners. I say to them, "Repent sinners!" You have not long to save your soul. If you think that I am not referring to you then you are mistaken. We are all sinners. It is the nature of men and women to sin. We must ask for forgiveness everyday and give up our sins. I, the *messenger*, am still a sinner even after all that I have seen and heard from God. And I tell you that if other sinners find me to be respectful of God and obeying his counsel not to sin, then they will more readily believe what I am. I am a servant of our Lord God, a *soldier in his temple* and a *messenger* of his new words. He has chosen to speak through me. I am only one human being among many millions. I am not worthy to carry my Lord's shoes, but he picks me, and he says to me, "Those who find the *messenger* will find thy Father." He means those who seek to understand what it is I am telling others and live their lives by the will of God, and then they will be ready for his saving grace. They have only to ask to be saved and God will bestow upon them the Holy Spirit and the life eternally on earth and heaven. Being saved is only the first step, because after a person receives his saving grace, he or she must seek the Lord's counsel everyday and walk as a new man or woman in Christ.

Family Responsibilities in the New Age

After a spouse has found God sometimes this unsettles the other spouse. After this, does your wife or family feel that they are losing you to God and that they will then not have you? I offer this advice. I see now that as a father gains a new son or daughter on the marriage of his child, so will your family gain a new Father in your family with ties to God. God is in now part of your family.

Family relationships must not be broken in God's namesake. If a father, mother, brother or sister shall sin, we should not participate with them.

But we should also not absolve them from the sin or our relationship. In their weakness they now need a strong family member to bring them back to the family as a good person. We should pray for them, and listen to them and be supportive. But we should not do things they ask of you if it is against God and his righteousness. We shall not judge them or think we are better, superior or above them. The path we chose is that we seek life, but the path they chose is that they seek death. In God there is not only a better life here on this earth, but there is also everlasting life in heaven. In sin there is death and the damnation of hell. If the family member chooses wealth and power on earth, they build a trap that condemns them. We shall not cut them off from the family. We shall grieve for our family member who has gone astray. Our compassion shall tell us that we grieve for those who sin and we wish to take care of their soul. We should always attempt to extend a hand and love them. We will not, however, partake of their sin. But above all, when they sin we will not let them dictate our actions or abuse us in anyway.

In God we place our trust. Should they disown us and cast us out so they may continue their sinning ways, we will be happy ourselves for we will know that we are very close to God. They would disown us because the evil in them cannot stand to be with the good in us. We shall grieve for that family member who has lost his or her way. The family must understand that this person who is part of the family is just as our arm is part of our body. We should not cut him or them off just as we would not cut our arm away from our body. The body is the family and the body is with the Temple of God. Those with Satan cannot stand to be with those who are godly and with God. For Jesus said they will persecute us in his namesake. Rejoice for we will be most holy. We will not cry for our loss but briefly. We will be glad for our gain and cry for their loss.

What should a father and mother do if their children sins and yet the parents be righteous. They shall not disown him or her. With a gentle love and assertive compassion they shall point the way to righteousness. They shall not withdraw, refuse to talk or absolve themselves from their child. The child shall be dear to those who are righteous and godly. They, however, will not let the child abuse them or allow themselves to stray from righteousness because of his or her sin(s). There shall always be a hand extended to them to show the child the light and the way to Jesus. You think that God hates and despises the sinners. I tell you he does not. He wants them to find righteousness and Jesus more than the parents do. Remember the child or the sinners have free will and must find God through their own eyes and heart. Then the spirit will truly be theirs. They will be righteous. I send a prayer for all those who need the gentle yoke of our Lord and that they find the way to the light.

Psalm 34:7 (King James Version)

"⁷The angel of the LORD encampeth round about them that fear him, and delivereth them."

Psalm 91:11 (King James Version)

"¹¹For he shall give his angels charge over thee, to keep thee in all thy ways."

Psalm 127:3 (King James Version)

"³Lo, children are a heritage of the LORD: and the fruit of the womb is his reward."

A Prayer for our Children

Our Father
Be it your will
Grant us a strong healthy child
To love and care for
We ask in Jesus namesake
We Praise Our Lord
Amen

CONCLUDING COMMENTS

I don't know what the future will bring regarding visions of angels and words from God. I have not seen an angel since 1997 at my step-father's funeral. I know I have seen many angels and heavenly persons and I have received many words from them. All these words of wisdom has helped me to be a better person and achieve more happiness than I ever thought possible. If I never see another angel I will not despair because I've got what I consider the whole story for mankind now and in the future to come. I will not resist God and his angels for they bring me only good things and more love in all forms. God's grace shall bless mankind for we are in his image and we are the temple which he most wants to be healthy and clean of sin.

Everyone knows there are very many wars fought all the time in this world and many persons die. However, many do not realize there is a much greater war. This war is across all countries of the world and it is being fought every day by every person in this world. It is the war between good and evil. The war between God and his numerous legions of angels and soldiers versus Satan and his demons is ongoing always. This is a much bigger war. We should never forget this for we could lose our souls to eternal damnation. This is a much bigger loss of humanity than a Christian being killed in war or any other situation of the world. I pray that more will keep their souls and be happy eternally. I also pray that families keep together and support each other in this world wide war.

My heavenly Father, I send this prayer to you with the blessing of Jesus Christ our savior. When anyone should question the merit of any man or woman as to whether they are worthy human beings I have this to say. Do not judge a man or woman by the color of his or her skin, or the church or beliefs he or she chooses to make theirs. Look at the ways they have of dealing with others. Do they love and treat their neighbors with honor and respect? Do they take care of their family and especially their children and grandparents? Do married persons treat each other with respect and dignity? If they do, then they are truly worthy of God's trust and their ways are truly good. God loves his children who are good. That is my prayer for humanity as the *messenger* for God and as the *"soldier in the Temple of God."* Be good so God may love you.
Amen.

By Dennis Wayne Schroll

AUTHOR BACKGROUND

Dennis Wayne Schroll is the son of Mary Ann Kimberling and the late Lewis Edward Kimberling (step-father) of Jamesport, Missouri. His birth father was Wayne Max Schroll. Dennis's father Wayne Max Schroll was killed in an airplane accident in Hutchinson, Kansas, April 4, 1948. He was taking pilot's training lessons. Dennis has brothers, Terry Schroll, Ronald Kimberling, Phillip Kimberling and sisters, Janet (Kimberling) Spencer, Natha (Kimberling) McAllister and Rebecca (Kimberling) Lang.

Dennis retired after 40 years of service in May, 2010 from the Aeronautical Systems Center, Wright-Patterson Air Force Base, which is near Dayton, Ohio. On April 30, 2010 the Department of the Air Force presented him with an Outstanding Civilian Career Service Medal and Award. The award was given to him in recognition of his distinguished performance in the support of the United States Air Force from June 23, 1970 to May 1, 2010 notably as a Senior Crew Systems Engineer, Aeronautical Systems Center, Air Force Material Command.

Mr. Schroll was a world recognized crew systems expert of nearly 40 years. His efforts resulted in the development, production and fielding of numerous advanced systems for the war fighter, enhancing the combat capability of the United States Air Force, Joint Services and Allied Nations. At his retirement ceremony he also received a medal for an Outstanding Career Service in Engineering for his past work which was primarily on military aircraft oxygen breathing systems. He was also awarded a medal for Outstanding Service for Combat Systems Program Office for aircraft night vision devices. The distinctive accomplishments of Mr. Schroll culminate a long and distinguished career with the United States Government and reflect great credit upon himself and the US Air Force.

Mr. Schroll was a 1964 graduate of the Tri-County High School in Jamesport, Missouri. He graduated as an Aerospace Engineer at the University of Missouri at Rolla, Rolla, Missouri in 1970 and distinguished himself being on the honor roll. He was immediately hired by the Aeronautical Systems Center, Wright-Patterson Air Force Base, Ohio where he served his entire career. Throughout his career he worked as a crew systems engineer on nearly every Air Force aircraft. He also supported numerous issues on Navy aircraft. He received his Master of Science Degree of Aeronautics & Astronautics at Ohio State University in 1978. He has received numerous awards for his outstanding performance in support of the Air Force mission.

He provided support to the following programs US Air Force and Navy programs:

- T-6A/B, B-1B, B-2, E-3, E-4 Presidential Aircraft, E-8 (Joint STARS), F-15, F-16, F-22, F-35, C-17, Life Support SPO, Peace Pearl, Senior Guardian, NASP, C-26, and C-27.
- He served on a special project that was directed by Congress to review the entire US Air Force (USAF) aircraft fleet to study conditions of all aircraft oxygen systems and he provided recommendations for improvements to all aircraft. This was then briefed to the Chief of Staff of the USAF and the Secretary of the USAF.
- Advisor and evaluator to source selections on T-46, C-17, Mission Support Aircraft, C-26, and Cruise Missile Mission Control Aircraft.

- Participated in the Executive Independence Review Teams including YA-7F, Joint STARS, CRAF AESS, AN/ALE-47, and C-17.
- Assigned to Special Investigations and tiger teams such as the investigation of the dusting from the B-1B oxygen concentrator and oxygen system hazards on the B-2 and other aircraft.
- Trained 20 civilian and military project engineers.
- Worked the UH-1 escape hatch, CH-3 instrument panel changes, UH-1N twin-engine helicopter developments, and PAVE LOW III Night Rescue helicopter.
- Worked the PAVE TACK Night Attack Program F-4 and F-111 crew station modifications for 5 years.
- Member of Joint Avionics Committee and Joint Task Flight Test Program.
- Assigned Strategic Systems on B-52 G/H Offensive Avionics System for 3 years.
- Assigned to the Airlift and Trainer System Program office and was a crew systems and life support evaluator for the C-17 Source Selection.
- Worked the Companion Trainer Aircraft and the H-X rescue helicopter.

His important professional experiences are as follows:

- Panel session leader numerous times at SAFE Symposium presented papers.
- He was the United States Air Force Delegate to North Atlantic Treaty Organization (NATO) Working Party for Compressed Gases for 28 years briefing United States position numerous times. He attended numerous meetings at NATO Headquarters and numerous times at other NATO countries.
- He was awarded an outstanding service plaque by the Italian Air Force. He was chairman of this NATO Panel for 8 years.

- He was awarded an outstanding NATO service certificate by the German Air Force
- He was an active member of Oxygen Standardization Coordinating Group, Principal United States Air Force Member for 19 years, and chairman for 7 years and he led many working panels within this group.
- He was an active member of Society of Automotive Engineering (SAE) Committee A-10 for commercial oxygen equipment. He developed 5 standards, one in widespread use and chaired many Ad Hoc groups for solving issues.
- He was a member of American Society of Testing and Materials (ASTM) Committee G-4 concerning design of safe oxygen systems for oxygen.
- He also taught courses for combustion hazards in aircraft oxygen systems, oxygen systems design course and ejections system course.

In addition to his duties as development and support engineer he performed above his required duties by being the author of 20 technical papers all presented at conferences. He was the author of three Technical Reports and 6 major development specifications. He was a co-author of an ASTM book used to teach oxygen safety throughout the world.

He had received numerous awards throughout his career including the following:

- Exemplary Civilian Service Medal December 2008 for work on T-6 Program
- 18 Performance Awards
- 2 Quality Salary Increase awards
- First Government Award for significant contributions for oxygen Standardization
- Service Award for Oxygen Standardization Coordination Group twice

- 4 Service Awards for the Society of Automotive Engineering Committee (SAE) for publishing standards documents
- Notable Achievement Award
- Suggestion Cash Award.

He is a member of the Grace United Methodist Church, Salem Avenue, Dayton, Ohio. He has also been a family member of the United Methodist Church in Jamesport, Missouri since he was a young child.